T0381175

FROM

THE LIFE AND TIMES

GRASS

OF

TO

PASTOR FITZ ALBERT "PAPPY" WATERMAN

GRACE

NIGEL WATERMAN

WESTBOW
PRESS®
A DIVISION OF THOMAS NELSON
& ZONDERVAN

WestBow Press books may be ordered through booksellers or by contacting:

WestBow Press
A Division of Thomas Nelson & Zondervan
1663 Liberty Drive
Bloomington, IN 47403
www.westbowpress.com
844-714-3454

ISBN: 979-8-3850-3023-1 (sc)
ISBN: 979-8-3850-3024-8 (e)

Library of Congress Control Number: 2024915375

Print information available on the last page.

WestBow Press rev. date: 11/06/2024

Dedication

This book is dedicated to Pappy and Mammy children and to their descendants in this generation and for generations to come.

Proceeds from the sale of this book will be given to the Fitz Albert Memorial Church for restoration and maintenance.

Acknowledgements

Special Thanks to

Mr. Haynesley Benn who provided encouragement as I wrote this book. He also provided advice and initially edited the manuscript. His love, admiration and respect for my dad is indeed profound. It is clear to me that my dad left an indelible mark on this gentleman.

My cousin Granville Bovell who provided invaluable research information. Born in 1932, he is the last standing eye witness to the construction and dedication of the church. His memory of details and events are astonishingly great. He provided verifiable information on the people and the process. He was my dad's nephew and when he spoke of "uncle", he spoke with reverence.

Foreword

Nigel Waterman's "Pappy" is a paean to his father Fitz Albert Waterman, whose life has been the defining inspiration for Nigel's own journey, which has not been without its own challenges.

However, it is much more than a double love story, Nigel's clear admiration for the man who loved his wife, Nigel and his nine siblings – Nigel being the last – and Pappy's remarkable love affair with the church.

Nigel captures life in Barbados from the early 1900s, taking readers through the social, educational and political challenges of the times. The book chronicles Pappy's progression from a plantation worker to working overseas and, in the end, establishing a church. It showed that he became a dominant and highly respected figure in the Mile and Quarter/Rose Hill/Maynard's/Ashton Hill area of St. Peter and Barbados as a whole.

That the writer is able to provide such historic and social context while exploring all aspects of his father's life in such a short book is a triumph, clearly indicating Nigel's understanding of the intertwining aspects of life on the individual and showing him to be a prescient observer of life at a young age; and, in the end, an excellent writer.

Above all, "Pappy" is about overcoming the odds and how ordinary people can make an extraordinary difference in their communities and in the life of those they encounter.

You will not only enjoy this book, but at the end of it, you will be motivated to reach for your goals. Any book that can do that is more than worthy of a read. Nigel Waterman's "Pappy" delivers.

Mackie Holder

Contents

1   The Beginning – As it was in the Beginning 1

2   All Saints Boys School 8

3   Reparations 14

4   Work Life 17

5   Marriage and Family Life...................................... 24

6   A New Chapter in Life - The Bethany
Christian Mission 35

7   Pappy's Vision and Purpose - Building the Church 38

8   A Journey Fulfilled - The Dedication 48

9   The Commitment - A New Beginning....................... 59

10 Church as it Happened....................................... 67

11 Revival Services at Home and Away 75

12 The service of Harvest Thanksgiving........................... 91

13 Church Excursions 94

14 Spiritual Experiences.. 98

15 Services of Thanksgiving for the lives of Pappy
and Mammy - So shall it be in the End 101

16 Special Honors - The Service to Unveil
Plaques / The Service to Rename the Church............... 113

17 Final Thoughts and Tributes 118

18 The Verdict of Those Who Sat at Pappy's Feet............ 123

Index... 129

CHAPTER 1

The Beginning – As it was in the Beginning

The Parish of St Peter Barbados is located in the northern section of the island. For generations, the people of St Peter considered it as both an urban and a rural Parish. On the western side of the Parish, the calm waters of the Caribbean Sea wash ashore. On this side lies Speightstown, the second largest town on the island and the main commercial hub for the northern parishes. A sizeable population of the parish reside in the west. In keeping with Barbados's tourism thrust, the western side also boast of luxury hotels and marinas.

The eastern side of the parish is rural; evidence of its sugar cane production past is still present. Situated in the midst of sugar cane fields and sugar cane plantations lies the community of French Village. Like most rural villages in Barbados, it evolved with its residents working in the sugar cane fields that surround it. Four Hill plantation is located to its east, Welch Town is located to its north, Mount Brevitor is located to its west and Orange Hill is located to its South. A historic sugar mill located five minutes to its East, stand as a sentinel to its sugar cane past.

On January 4, 1915, my father, Fitz Albert Waterman "Pappy," was born in French village. He was the last child and only boy of his mother's three children. His grandmother, Elizabeth Waterman and his mother Mary Magdeline Waterman were also born in French Village. His grandfather, Fitz C Walker from whom his name is derived, and his father, Samuel "Poor Boy" Walker, were both born ten minutes to the East at Four Hill, St Peter.

Pappy's grandparents and parents all worked in the sugar cane fields that surrounded their home. His father Samuel rose to become a Supervisor at Four Hill plantation where he worked. Given the existing social and economic factors of the day, that was a considerable achievement. When asked about where he worked and grew into adulthood, Samuel remarked that, "canes surrounded us, and there was no place to go and nothing else to do." This statement summarized the situation in 1915, the year of Pappy's birth.

In 1915, the sugar industry employed 90 percent of Barbados's inhabitants and contributed 90 percent to the island's economy. In fact, 99 percent of all arable land in Barbados supported sugar cane cultivation. It is widely acknowledged that sugar cane production was King on the island until major diversification projects took place starting ostensibly as late as the 1970's.

Soon after Pappy was born, his mother moved to Mount Brevitor, a village twenty minutes by foot to the west of French Village. She left French Village to escape a marauding bookkeeper. The bookkeeper had sired several children in the village. Biracial children were present everywhere and everyone in the community knew they were his children. This bookkeeper had pursued her relentlessly to the point of harassment, so she left French Village.

Once in Mount Brevitor, Pappy's mother was fortunate to move to a piece of land owned by Mrs. Padmore who owned a single plot of land. Mount Brevitor was part plantation tenantry, and part freehold landowners. Mrs. Padmore's plot became vacant because she had moved to Panama to join her husband who had gone to work on the Panama Canal. She would eventually invite

Pappy's sister Carlotta "Lottie" Cox to join them in that Central American nation.

Lottie lived in Panama for about five years and then returned to Barbados. She described it as a hard place to live. She did not describe or define hard in anyway. All she knew was that conditions seemed hard for the many people from the Caribbean who had done backbreaking and dangerous work on the Canal. Construction of the Panama Canal ended in 1914. After its completion, employment opportunities diminished for many people of the Caribbean. Mr. Padmore worked as a pipe fitter, and was fortunate to survive the diseases and accidents that killed an estimated 22,000 men. After the canal's construction, his income spiralled downwards. However, it is not clear what made it hard for Lottie. Questioned on many occasions, she never volunteered the answers. What she said repeatedly was that she came back home to Barbados and the love of her St Peter family.

After living at Mount Brevitor for almost three years, Pappy's mother moved her chattel house to Benn's Hill, St Peter. Whilst living on the Padmore's property, the Padmore family offered the land for sale to Pappy's mother. The Waterman family could not afford to purchase the land, so they moved to rental property at Benn's Hill. Pappy's grandmother Elizabeth joined them soon afterward. She moved to support her daughter in providing for her children, but also for comfort and love.

Pappy and the boys of Benn's Hill explored their surroundings. They visited a nearby cave where they examined paintings experts concluded were carved by the Arawaks, the first aboriginal people. Arawaks lived on the island of Barbados between the periods 800 to 1200 A.D.

Pappy and his friends also explored the gully that ran to the back or South of the village. This gully was part of a fissure in the land that ran from East of Benn's Hill to its West. In the months when there was heavy rainfall, the gully served as a natural drainage system. Rivers of water flowed through its passage, transporting debris in its path. The local people referred to this movement of water as "de gully out."

After the move to Benn's Hill, Pappy's family attended All Saints Anglican church. His grandmother, one of the few women that could read, served as a lieutenant in All Saints Church Army. In the ensuing years, Pappy accompanied her everywhere she went. His role was to carry her heavy Bible.

The move to Benn Hill and attending All Saints Anglican Church was a miniscule step up the social mobility ladder. Prior to moving to Benn's Hill, Pappy's grandmother and his mother had attended the small wooden Pentecostal church in French Village. Pappy's grandmother had attended this church as a young woman and her daughter had followed suit. The local people had built this church. They used their ingenuity and pooled their meagre resources to construct this meeting place. Their Pastor came from and lived within the community.

Service to God was paramount in the lives of the people who attended this church. Worship included a singing of songs, in an upbeat rhythmic joyful manner. Hand clapping and dancing formed an essential part of the worship. Everyone regarded these acts as rejoicing in the Lord. The preaching was an animated and passionate exposition of the teachings of the Bible. During the sermons, the congregation would participate, responding with shouts of amen or providing encouragements with exclamations of "preach pastor" or "hallelujah." The church provided not just a place to worship, but also a place where you wore your best clothing; called your "Sunday go to meeting clothing." It also provided a place of respite from the worries and labors of the day. Once at church, memories of their standard of living, or problems working the fields were lost in worship and fellowship with their other saints.

French Village Pentecostal Church

In contrast, All Saints Anglican church was an imposing stone building erected in 1649 on lands once owned by Pleasant Hall plantation. The proceeds of slavery and slave labor had significantly contributed to its construction and maintenance.

Originally, it was the worship and burial place for the plantation owners. It served the owners and their families from the surrounding plantations of Pleasant Hall, Ebworth, Portland, Four Hill, Mount Brevitor and Welch Town to name a few. The British historian Richard Ligon, who lived in Barbados from 1647 to 1650, reported that All Saints was an imposing church and one of the earliest churches built of stone.

All Saints Anglican Church

The worship at All Saints mirrored that of the other Anglican Churches in England. Unenergetic organ playing to slow impassive singing was the order of the church worship. From its inception until the 1960's, the priests came from Britain, and wore long white robes. They read from prepared text found in "The Book of Common Prayers." It was widely observed that their sermons did not exceed fifteen minutes in duration. This practice has persisted into modern times. Many friends of this writer who attended All Saints described the preaching as uninspiring. One said that he did not understand the various rituals and chants that he saw and heard during worship.

After All Saints Church was first consecrated; it took at least another 240 years for black people to attend for worship. By 1915, there was a trickle into the church. By the time the first black officiating priest was ordained in 1937, the trickle of black congregants had risen to a flood. The fact that historically it was not available to the black population, made it appear to be a step up from the local village church. In addition, the somber organ harmonies, British priests and their accents, long white robes, and the uniformed manner of the structure of the services, appealed to the black population. These factors brought them closer to the way plantation owners worshipped, and vicariously, closer to these folk. To this day, some people still view attending All Saints Church as a symbol of class and status.

CHAPTER 2

All Saints Boys School

Pappy first attended All Saints Boys Primary School in 1919. Built of stone in 1647, it was located on a rocky piece of land unsuitable for sugar cane cultivation. As was the case of the church, Pleasant Hall Plantation once owned the land. The school and the church have similar histories. They are located within close proximity and they both benefitted from the proceeds of slavery, and built with slave labor. The school's original mission was to provide a primary education to the children of the nearby plantation owners.

When Pappy attended All Saints Boy School, the churches administered elementary schools in Barbados. The island's legislature recognized these schools. In 1900, the Barbados Legislature regulated, and uniformed fees payable to primary schools. The fees ranged from one pence to three pence per week. In 1919, Pappy's fee was one pence per week. The teachers collected the fees directly from the pupils in their charge.

In 1919, Mr. Cumberbatch was the name of Pappy's headmaster. He lived in Speightstown, which was located, a mile and three quarters to the west of the school. He rode to school in a horse and buggy. The buggy had one seat for the driver and one for a passenger. It did not have a top to cover from the rain or the sun. In those days, Barbadians called the buggy a "Trala" buggy. Every school day, Mr. Cumberbatch sent pupils he held responsibility for to the grounds of the nearby church to cut grass to feed the horse. He also sought out pupils to fill a large container with water to enable the horse to drink. The headmaster tethered the horse to a stake in the ground, where it drank and ate the grass for the duration of the school day.

In the same year of 1919, All Saints Boys Primary School classes on average comprised of ten students. Daily, teachers taught the children the alphabet and the pronunciation of words. Teachers wrote on boards and asked the children to write on their slates what they saw on the board. The teacher came around to each student to see if the boys had correctly copied the written assignment. If a student copied incorrectly, the teacher spanked him and the boy would cry. Pappy did not have a slate because his mother did not provide the funds for him to buy one; therefore, he did not copy the written material from the board. Like other boys in his class without a slate, Pappy's teacher directed him to stand at the back of the class and watch the proceedings. The teacher paid no more attention to these boys.

Several of Pappy's classmates incorrectly copied the written assignment, and suffered the consequences. Corporal punishment played an integral role in the discipline of children during that era. Total strangers could spank a child if they saw the child misbehaving in public. This punishment was usually done by a woman, who would remark that "you should go home and tell your mother why you were spanked, and who did the spanking." If the child did tell his mother, that would subject him to another flogging. If a neighbor saw the mother and told her that the child had misbehaved, a spanking would follow. The entire community cared and took part in the upbringing of their children.

The teachers at All Saints Boys sent their charges to the Headmaster when they committed serious offences. The most serious of which was not having their school fee. In 1923, teacher's pay came from the fees directly collected from the boys. In 1923, the headmaster at All Saints Boys School literally threw Pappy out of the school for not having his school fee. One Monday morning as usual, the teacher called the class roll and when he got to Pappy, he called out, "Fitz Waterman". Pappy answered with the regular reply of "present please," but remained seated at his desk. It was the practice to take your penny to the teacher when it was your turn at the roll call.

When Pappy did not walk to the teacher's desk, the teacher knew immediately, that another pupil did not have the school fee.

The teacher summoned the Headmaster, Mr. Cumberbatch to his class. Without speaking, he walked to the desk where Pappy sat and grabbed him by the back of the neck. He then walked him briskly to the school door and pushed him down the long steep steps of the school. He then yelled instructions to him; "Go home and tell your mother to send the school fees."

The boys who witnessed these weekly occurrences simply laughed. They laughed because of their innocence, and because the implications of these acts were far beyond their comprehension.

At seven years of age, Pappy left school about 9.00 am on that fateful day and waited until 5.00 pm when his mother came home from work. He told his mother what happened, and she replied that she did not have the penny. He did not go back to school, that was the end of his formal education.

This happened to several boys during that period. There are no official records but several senior citizens estimated that about 40 - 50 percent of the boys in 1923 forfeited their education because of non-payment of fees. Some boys left school as early as eight years of age to look after siblings. This allowed their parents to work.

In addition, some boys had to leave school to go to work. They went to work in the third gang, a group made up of children who worked on the sugar plantations. Some boys went to school until they were fourteen years of age. That was a rarity in rural

Barbados. In fact, Barbadian society deemed these boys fortunate, given the existing socio-economic conditions.

The act of throwing Pappy out of All Saints Boys School in 1923 was an insensitive and brutal act. Pappy's ancestors came from Four Hill and Mount Brevitor plantations respectively. The owners of these plantations helped financed the school for their children to attend. The blood and sweat of Pappy's ancestors poured out, to procure the money and labor for this school. The question then, is; should their descendent not benefit from their labors? Pappy's teachers knew, or ought to have known about the prevailing economic and social conditions. They knew, or ought to have known, that their society was emerging from slavery. They knew or ought to have known, that whereas the plantation owners were collectively paid five million pounds for the loss of chattel, the people (chattel) were set adrift from the plantations empty handed and left to fend for themselves. Given these facts, how could they be so insensitive to a seven-year-old boy who came from this society?

When this writer attended All Saints Boys School forty years later, (1963 – 1970) the social economic situation had improved considerably. In fact, primary school education was free since 1944, and secondary education since 1961. In addition, since the establishment of the University of the West Indies in 1948, the government of Barbados has paid the tuition fees for its citizens attending the university.

Despite this improvement, there was still widespread poverty in the rural catchment areas of the school. When I attended, teachers were keen to assist poorer boys. Teachers bought shoes, pencils and books amongst other things from their own pockets and provided lunch to those that did not have. Some of the boys given assistance, graduated to senior roles in Barbados and beyond its border. They excelled in the public, private and non - profit sectors. An enduring question for this writer is; what if Pappy had receive assistance from his teachers?

Pappy's teachers of 1923 were also the descendants of slaves, but their job had provided them a tiny step on the social mobility ladder. Their job, and a perception of upward mobility, had given them a pretext to forget, rather conveniently, their past. Their quest to be paid and selfish pride far outweighed feelings of empathy for the less fortunate. The maintenance of his horse and buggy mattered more to the Head Master than educating boys. This luxury vehicle of the day was a status symbol that had catapulted him into the realm of the petty bourgeoisie. Incentivized to maintain this lifestyle, the fees became the priority, and consequently; had to be paid.

The act of pushing Pappy down the stairs was brutal in the extreme. The physical act itself was jarring for a boy of seven years old. Pappy never forgot the trauma of that rainy Monday. He had forgiven those that perpetrated the act, but never forgot the consequences he faced from the action taken.

That act cast a child adrift to a world, which condemned him to menial labor. With no job skills, and no training for the society in which he would inhabit, what was he supposed to do? Having to leave school at seven affected him for the rest of his life. It set him back a substantial distance behind the starting line, from where others in his community started. It grossly impeded his ability to acquire assets and his ability to pass on those assets to future generations. It is therefore clear that the setback also affected subsequent generations of his children, grandchildren and great grandchildren.

All Saints Boys School

CHAPTER 3

Reparations

In Barbados, the political leadership and academics have championed the quest for reparations for the descendants of slaves. Successive Prime Ministers have repeatedly said that the topic of reparations must be the focus of discussions at the highest levels. The Prime Minister of Barbados travelled to the island of St Vincent on September 15, 2013 to unveil a plan, demanding reparations from Britain and other British establishments that profited from slavery. Following that meeting, The Caribbean Community Secretariat, of which Barbados is a founding member, established The Caribbean Reparations Commission. The Commission's mandate is to seek a path for reparations for the peoples of the Caribbean.

Is it naïve to suggest that the Barbados government and the Anglican Diocese of Barbados jointly owe an apology and reparations to Pappy's descendants?

Pappy was physically assaulted, humiliated and suffered a lifelong indignity from the hands of his teachers.

The actions of his teachers brought emotional and physical damage.

The actions of his teachers significantly curtailed his standing in the community, his earning potential and his standard of living.

These facts support my contention:

In 1919 when Pappy attended All Saints Boys School, the Anglican Church of Barbados administered elementary schools. The Barbados government provided funding.

In 1846, the Barbados Legislature made a state grant for education purposes.

In 1850, the Barbados Legislature passed the first Education Act. In addition, The Legislature increased the Education Grant by 3000 pounds.

In 1858, a New Education Act provided for a full time Inspector of Schools.

In 1874, the annual grant to education increased to 9,200 pounds.

In 1878, a New Education Act fixed the education grant to 15,000 pounds annually.

In 1900, the Legislature officially recognized elementary schools.

In 1944, elementary school teachers became Civil Servants.

The above data showed that the government of Barbados, over the ensuing years after slavery contributed financially, and enacted laws for the administration of schools and education in general. In addition, the government of Barbados rightfully took full control of the administration of education, and therefore the assets and liabilities that came with that control.

Stare decisis or precedent is a principal in Common Law Jurisdictions like Barbados and Canada. The following precedent bolsters my contention that the Barbados government, and the Anglican Church of Barbados, owe reparations to Pappy's descendants.

In the early part of the 20th century, the government of Canada financed schools administered mainly by the Roman Catholic Church. The main goal of these schools was to assimilate Indigenous Peoples to the European way of life. The Catholic brothers and nuns abused the children, some died from abuse and neglect. They initiated policies to strip the natives of their identity and practices. These policies scarred Indigenous people for life.

Native Canadian organizations sought reparations for the wrongs their children suffered. Following a settlement agreement, the Catholic Church paid 54 million dollars in restitution to various native organizations.

In 2006, the Canadian government recognized the damaged done by residential schools and agreed to pay a 20-billion-dollar compensation package.

Given the above, it is my contention that compensation in the two-to-ten-million-dollar range should accrue to Pappy's descendants. I submit that the Anglican Diocese of Barbados is liable for ten percent of this compensation and the government of Barbados ninety percent.

CHAPTER 4

Work Life

Out of school, and only seven years of age, Pappy went to work for Colleton plantation in the parish of St Lucy. Colleton plantation was a forty -minute walk from Pappy's house. The plantation wanted boys to lead cattle out of their pens and into the fields to plough. Yoked with ploughs, the cattle ploughed the land on a straight line. The pay was $0.08 a day or $0.40 a week. After three years of leading cattle, Pappy left Colleton.

After leaving Colleton, he went to work at White Hall plantation in the parish of St Peter with the third gang. White Hall plantation was a twenty- minute walk from his house in Benn's Hill. During slavery, the plantations implemented a gang system to distinguish its workers. There were three gangs, the first, the second and the third gang. The first gang workers were apportioned the harder work; these were the better able workers. The second gang was for less abled workers like the elderly and teenagers. The third gang comprised of children, Hence, the plantation owners assigned to this group the easiest work.

At White Hall. Ms. Lena Toppin led the third gang that Pappy joined. She treated the youth with kindness and love. Within months of working in the third gang, it was time to harvest the sugar canes. Pappy's brother-in-law Ben Welch recommended to his supervisor that Pappy lead the mule carts that transported the sugar canes to Heymans sugar factory. The pay was $0.14 a day, which was a significant promotion at the time. The next year the pay increased to $0.20 a day.

In 1935, Ethiopia was engaged in a war with Italy. Italy's Emperor Mussolini had invaded Ethiopia in a bid to colonize the country. Ethiopia's Haile Selassie employed his troops to repel the invasion. Pappy would come home from his job at White Hall, to listen to the daily British Broadcasting Corporation (BBC) reports of the war. He joined a group of people from the Mile and a Quarter community, who gathered around the community grocery store. The Brathwaite family owned this store, and they made their gramophone available to the community.

People in Barbados were on Selassie's side and hoped that he would defeat Mussolini. In June 1936, Selassie gave a speech to the League of Nations. He spoke in English and requested assistance for his people. Pappy said that the BBC played the speech many times. He said that Selassie was passionate and the way he spoke one had to listen until the end. Pappy also remembered that Selassie gave a speech in 1936 that ended with these words "when my eyes are dry others eyes would be wet." He believed those words to be prophetic because three years later, World War two broke out.

World War two gave Pappy an opportunity to go to the United States to work. In 1943, he travelled to Hoopeston Illinois, to work for Hoopeston Canning Company, a large corn canning operation. He worked for this company for three months before he moved to the state of Wisconsin to work at a factory making gunpowder to support the war efforts.

Pappy relayed that the training given on the machines that churned out the gunpowder was inadequate. He said that one had to learn quickly on their own. He said that he oversaw a machine that mixed materials for the final product. It took a minute and a half to fully charge and then took three and a half minutes to rotate as it mixed the material. At the end of the rotation, the machine sounded an alarm and a blue light came on. After the blue light came on, he pressed a green led button, and the material moved down a shaft to another processing station. Pappy worked at this plant for five months before a disagreement took place that forced him to move on.

A supervisor wanted him at the end of the day's shift to go down to the basement and hose down gun powder drippings. Pappy resisted this because where he worked in the factory was hot and this heat elicited a great amount of sweat. For this reason, he was not interested in going down to the damp and dark basement with water. In addition, he reasoned and voiced to the supervisor that he was on his own. If he became ill, there was no one to take care of him. The supervisor said that a hospital existed in the city and that the company would provide the transport to get him there if he became ill.

His immediate supervisor summoned another supervisor to explain the hosing system. The summoned supervisor said that dry air came out of the nozzle of a hose, and not water. Despite this new explanation, Pappy still resisted going down to the basement. As punishment for refusing to go down to the basement, there were consequences. Their supervisor unilaterally changed the job status for Pappy and three other Barbadian colleagues who had resisted.

The pay working in the factory was $1.09 an hour; the supervisor transferred the Barbadians to a job transporting the finished product to transport trains. Transport workers earned $0.80 an hour.

Pappy and his three Barbadian counterparts asked the Liaison Officer for the Jamaican workers to intervene on their behalf. The Liaison Officer told the supervisor that the Barbadian workers were right not to move from the factory floor to the basement at the end of the working day. He argued that these were two different roles. He said workers should be hired specifically to hose down the drippings given the large volume at the end of the day. He pressed for their reinstatement. Given the acrimony that had emerged, the Barbadians decided to leave this factory, it was time to move on.

The Jamaican Liaison officer arranged for Pappy and his fellow Barbadians to move to Peru, Indiana to work in a peaches canning factory. Pappy worked for eleven months in Indiana. After eleven months had expired, it was the end of World War two and the end of his work contracts.

After the working section of the contracts were completed, many Barbadians severed the intent of the entire contracts, and branched out on their own. These men intended to work illegally, and at some point marry an American citizen and acquire a Green Card for Permanent Residency. Whilst in Indiana, a proposal was offered to Pappy that he stay in America. An American woman, who worked at the canning factory, told him that he could stay in America, work, and send money to Barbados for his four daughters. She said she would ask her brother-in-law to allow Pappy to work with him. Her brother-in-law worked driving trains transporting goods across the USA. She assured him that law enforcement personnel did not stop the trains.

Pappy brought this proposal to the attention of other older Barbadian colleagues. He wanted to solicit their opinions. Several colleagues had already absconded, and amongst those remaining, the topic of to stay or to go was constantly discussed. His colleagues told him that to work and send home money was a good idea, but it was a serious risk to undertake. They said if stopped by the police without immigration documents, his return to Barbados would be swift. There will be no opportunity to collect any personal belongings.

With this information in hand, with a commitment to God and his wife, and his church, and with four children to parent, Pappy headed back to Barbados to his family. He had spent two years in America. He came back to Barbados and to more agricultural work.

He went back to Warleigh Plantation in the parish of St. Peter where he worked digging cane holes out of harvest time and cutting canes at harvest time. On average, he earned $0.30 per day digging cane holes. At harvest time, the pay was substantially higher.

In 1959, Barbados moved from the vestry system of local government to District Councils. The vestry system had existed since 1745 and in 1958 with the passage of The Local Government Act the vestry system ended. This act divided the island into three Districts, the Northern District, the Southern District and The City of Bridgetown. The Local Government Act incorporated the Parish of St Peter into the Northern District Council.

Pappy's brother-in-law Eustace "Sonny" Murphy won the contest to become Superintendent of Works for the Northern District Council. This also occurred in 1959. Council members won their seats on a mandate to transform the gravel and marled roads, off the main roads of the north; to paved ones. It was widely acknowledged, that gravel and marl roads were inconvenient and created accessibility problems. Medical personnel also argued that they were also health hazards. Rural folk who travelled these roads and walked barefooted were plagued with chiggers that entered their calloused and fissured feet. Affected people from St Peter travelled to The St Peter Alms House in Speightstown for treatment. To treat this condition nurses used hot needles to burn and kill the chiggers.

Pappy's brother-in-law hired him to work in road construction. He assigned him to a crew that worked near his home. Hired as a laborer, his pay was $ 0.27 a day. The crew built and paved roads that led to villages that were located off the main roads. They built a main road from Speightstown to the northern village of Six Mens. Even though there were no significant excavations, each stretch of road presented different challenges for the workers. The Speightstown to Six Men's Village Road, which ran parallel to the Caribbean Sea coastline, was sandy at the beginning and throughout the entire stretch. This road required much gravel and concrete compacting to strengthen it. Side streets off the Speightstown to Mile and a Quarter main road, were surveyed to ascertain that the road followed the land designated for road building purposes. The gravel that overlaid these roads provided a good foundation for asphalt paving.

Pappy worked for the Northern District Council until 1967 at the onset of its phasing out process. The 1961 – 1966 administration of Prime Minister Errol Barrow disestablished the Council system. The offices of the District Councils and the Mayor were made redundant.

The phasing out process took from 1967 – 1969. Meanwhile in 1963, Pappy's supervisor had noticed his work ethic and had recommended his promotion to the role of Supervisor to another crew. His brother-in-law Sonny Murphy; the Superintendent interviewed him. In the end, he had to forego the promotion; he was unable to record adequately the delivery of gravel by the trucks, amongst other recording duties. That single act would motivate him to rectify that shortcoming.

After the disbandment of the District Councils, local matters transferred to the national level. Constituents of the various parishes had to depend on their parliamentary representatives to have provisions or services performed.

With the Councils' assignment at an end, Pappy went back to agriculture. He went to work for Orange Hill Plantation. It was the sugar cane planting season, and he worked digging cane holes at $0.12 per hundred. Some workers were very proficient at this skill so to slow the process down the plantation allotted 300 cane holes a day or $0.36 a day.

Pappy left Orange Hill after a short stint and went back to Warleigh plantation. At Orange Hill, the management wanted cane holes dug deeper than the normally accepted depths. In addition, at Warleigh he could finish work at 3.00 pm. He could then hurry home, and work until the sun went down at 6.00

pm. He worked on a small piece of land situated at the back of his house at Mile and a Quarter. The land produced a variety of vegetables for his family and neighbors.

Pappy worked for Rayside Construction Company, a road-building contractor for the last ten years of his working life. He retired from the world of work in 1983.

CHAPTER 5

Marriage and Family Life

Pappy was living at lower Mile and Quarter when he met Myrtle Richards. He had seen her several times and admired her. When he eventually approached her for a conversation, she was unable to talk to him in public. She was a member of All Saints Anglican Church and was on their confirmation class. In the 1930's, girls in confirmation classes were forbidden to talk to boys. If a girl was caught talking to a boy, she was removed from the class. This brought about great shame and humiliation in the community for the girl and her family.

Pappy had to wait until after confirmation classes before he had a conversation about a relationship. The conversation occurred after they both attended Lisle Hendy's wedding ceremony. Lisle Hendy was a member of the Mile and a Quarter community. His wedding took place at All Saints Anglican Church in 1933. After the ceremony, Pappy was able to approach Myrtle and profess his admiration and love.

Fitz Albert Waterman "Pappy" and Myrtle Jestine Waterman "Mammy" were married August 11, 1935. The ceremony took place at The Mason Hall Christian Mission Church, located in St. Michael Barbados, an hour's drive from their Mile and a Quarter residences. Franco "Franka" Edwards a Mile and a Quarter resident chauffeured the couple back and forth on their wedding day.

Once married, the young couple moved to a small chattel house Pappy built which was also in lower Mile and a quarter. Six months after marriage, the couple built an extension to the house.

In 1948, Rose Hill plantation, located about ten minutes by foot from where Pappy lived at Mile and a Quarter, was divesting most of its land to create house lots (called house spots in 1948 Barbados). Pappy bought a regular sized lot for forty -two pounds sterling.

When Pappy bought the lot, Barbados was a British colony and the government of Barbados established the pound in 1948 as the official currency to replace the Barbados dollar. The official currency changed again in 1951 to the Eastern Caribbean Currency. In 1972, with the establishment of the Barbados Central Bank, a new Barbados currency was established.

The purchase of that land was a wise and forward- thinking act. It was the foresight of two minds, working in unison. Two minds that saw the pride and long-term benefits of land ownership. What made it so thoughtful a purchase is the fact that at the time of acquisition, for Pappy and Mammy, this was a daunting task. On average, they earned a combined forty- five cents per day or $2.25 a week or annually $108.00. The land was valued at Barbados $1512.00. This total without interest equalled fourteen times their annual wages.

With savings from his American trip, Pappy and Mammy deposited an amount that exceeded that required by the mortgagor. The Government of Barbados Savings Bank was the mortgagor for this land.

In 1980, Pappy received a notice of payment due, from the Barbados National Housing Corporation. The invoice stated, "Fitz Albert Waterman and Myrtle Jestine Waterman jointly owed $180.00 for a parcel of land vested at Rose Hill, St Peter." The National Housing Corporation were transferred mortgages from the now defunct Government Savings Bank. This payment, thirty- two years after the purchase, was the last payment made for that mortgage.

Soon after the land purchase in 1948, Pappy moved his chattel house to his Rose Hill spot. After setting up his house, he transformed his plot by planting sugar canes, fruit trees and a variety of vegetables. Sugar cane cultivation generated much needed income. Every year Pappy harvested the sugar canes and sold them to the nearby Heymans Sugar Factory, where they were processed.

Whereas sugar cane cultivation supplemented his income, planting fruit trees were for food consumption. Trees planted included papaya, banana, coconut, avocado pear, mango, and lime. These trees supplied his family and neighbors with fresh fruit throughout the year.

Pappy cultivated his vegetable garden with thyme, lettuce, corn, sweet potatoes, cassava, pumpkins and okra to name a few. These vegetables also supplied his household and his neighbors with fresh produce.

In 1970, Pappy upgraded the house to a mixture of stone and wood. He renovated the wooden front section of the house, to blend with the new expansion of the building. To allow for the expansion of other rooms, the builders eliminated some rooms from the renovated wooden house.

The expansion of the rest of the house with red brick blocks followed a growing trend of using this material. David Gibbons a man from the surrounding Ashton Hall community supervised the renovation and building project. A master mason, he drew the building plans for the project, and recommended the red blocks. The main component of these blocks was sand acquired from the adjacent parish of St Andrew. This sand was dissimilar to sand found around the beaches of Barbados. Experts have concluded that over millennia, this sand had blown across the Atlantic Ocean from the Sahara Desert. It had accumulated in the eastern Parish of St. Andrew, where the Atlantic Ocean wash ashore. Property owners mined and kilned this sand for building purposes.

Painting of Pappy's House 1975

To assist in the renovation and building project, two other highly skilled artisans supported David Gibbons. Sylvan "Born Drunk" Griffith worked as a mason and Elridge "Rack a Light" Chandler a carpenter.

Although David Gibbons supervised the building project, the artisans individually negotiated their pay. Gibbons and Griffith said what they were charging weekly for their services. With this knowledge, Pappy was able to budget their wages into his expenditures. On the other hand, Chandler opted for what many said was a dishonest ploy. When Pappy asked him what he was charging for the weeks' work, he told Pappy that he should pay him what he thought he was worth. It is unclear if his ploy worked in his favor or not. Pappy paid him exactly what he paid Griffith. When Pappy eventually told Gibbons about Chandler's payment tactics, Gibbons expressed surprise at his actions. Gibbons thought it was a strategy to deceive. He told Pappy it was correct to pay him the same as Griffith. Gibbons promised Pappy that for future jobs he would seek other people for carpentry roles.

The road that passes by Pappy's house, leads to Maynard's Plantation to the West. In the ensuing years, the official address of the property remained Rose Hill. However, because of where the road leads, it is known popularly, as Maynard's Road.

Everyone who knew the Waterman family acknowledged that the Maynard's Road residence is the cradle of the family clan. The family footprint is as permanent as the road that passes through it. The respect Pappy and Mammy garnered in the community imprinted their footprints. People often came up to Pappy in the streets to relay a complaint or unburden a worry and seek advice.

In addition, the pair laid down deep roots in the community with the children borne from this union. For generations to come, the home he established at Maynard's Road where his children grew, will be known as Pappy's house. On several occasions, Pappy insisted that when he was gone, the house must remain the family house. He emphasized that no one child should lay claims to it. He reiterated that maintaining the house should be the task of all his children and after his children his grandchildren. He envisioned that his descendants at home or abroad would have a place to come home to for relaxation or to convalesce.

Pappy's vision for his house has not materialized. One of his sons has claimed it as his own. In addition, it has become an unwelcome place for his children and grandchildren to visit. One of his sons has argued that he initiated repairs to the house and therefore it belonged to him. His unilateral declaration has angered most of his siblings and a large percentage of his nephews and nieces. They speak amongst themselves but are not interested in any course of action.

It must be emphasized that Pappy's son did not singularly repair the house. He contributed the greatest amount when you consider the skills and labor he employed to complete the project. It should be a given that if a child has the skills to repair the house, then the child would take the lead in the repair. That lead should not be the principal reason to claim ownership. It is indeed commendable for one to lead in initiating repairs to the house. It is also noteworthy to establish some semblance of order and direction when everything appears to be in abeyance. However, declaring ownership shifts Pappy's universal family concept in the opposite direction. One fundamental way the direction shifts, lies in what happens with future repairs. If a child proclaims ownership, it follows then, that it would make it very difficult to solicit funds from other siblings for future repairs or upgrades to the property.

Pappy's son also installed one of Pappy's granddaughters to occupy the house without seeking the opinion of most of his siblings. If he had done due diligence, he would have realized that this granddaughter did not visit Pappy and Mammy when they were alive. In fact, she had not been to Pappy's house for several years even though she lived in St Peter, Barbados.

Once installed, this granddaughter has exhibited behavior unwelcoming to some of Pappy's children and grandchildren. A sullen, mute demeanor greet those arriving at the house. An atmosphere of "you are encroaching on my space" pervades. In addition, she has repeatedly lied, conveying false messages to the purported owner about issues surrounding visitors to Pappy's house. To some of Pappy's descendants, visiting Maynard's Road has become a jarring and uncomfortable experience.

Pappy did not leave a written will, so; according to the law of the land, he died intestate. However, it would be wrong to say that his surviving spouse and children did not know his wishes. His oft-repeated vision for his house was his will. If the sibling who claims ownership of the property was reasonable, and had any respect for Pappy's legacy, he would have honored Pappy's will, and acted as he directed. His actions are illegal and shows ignorance of the Law of Succession in Barbados.

The Barbados Succession Act, Cap 249, mandates that if you die intestate, your property will be distributed as follows:

If you have a spouse and children:

Your spouse is entitled to one-third of the estate and the remainder goes to the children in equal shares.

Pappy's spouse also passed on, it follows then, to acquiesce to the spirit of the Barbados Succession Act then her one - third portion remains in the estate. It also follows, that equity is the principle in the Barbados Succession Act. The principle of equity demands that the property in equal parts belong to his children. In other words, each of his children are entitled to ten percent of the property.

Pappy's children are not interested in having the property sold and divided. Some are aware it would require someone filing for a grant of Letters of Administration. An official document issued by the Court, which signifies the conferral by the Court on a named administrator, or named administrators of legal authority, enabling him or them to administer the deceased's estate. They all recognize that the legal costs are an insurmountable barrier, but more importantly, that it would go against Pappy's wishes.

The ongoing impasse begs the questions, why claim ownership to an asset that you cannot sell or bequeath to another? Who or what legal entity provided the authority to say boldly to one of Pappy's daughters that she cannot go to Pappy's house. Where did he gain the power to order a grandchild to leave the house where he was temporarily residing, until repairs were completed to the grandchild's house? Can one amass benefits, by holding on to the conveyancing documents for Pappy's house? What gains are to be made when the documents of the Church at Mile and a Quarter, remain in the custody of someone other than the Pastor of the church?

The answers point to a disregard for what is legal and just. It shows a total disrespect for the spirit of Pappy's intentions, and the legacy that he willed to his descendants. It points to a craving for the right to make decisions, to be the leader. It shows a yearning to be able to impose sanctions that authority allows its holders to impose.

The ownership of the house and the matter of the occupant of the house must be resolved. Left unresolved, in thirty to forty years, the property would mirror many "family houses" in Barbados. These houses are abandoned and are in states of disrepair for several reasons. One reason there is abandonment, is that there is no individual owner. Ownership is in abeyance, and the descendants cannot be bothered individually or collectively with the legal costs and the accompanying stress necessary to formalize the ownership. In addition, as time progresses, descendants often start their families. They have their purchased properties to maintain. This causes preferences to shift. The descendant's property gains the ascendancy and their parent's property declines in level of importance.

Pappy was aware that properties left to siblings are often abandoned and fall into disrepair. He thought those abandonments were a waste and indeed shameful. He strongly believed that his house would not suffer the same fate.

I believe Pappy would have been pleased that his house underwent repairs and renovations. I also believe that he would be happy that there is an occupant. However, what would cause much pain is the fact that a declaration of persona non grata extends to one of his daughters. In addition, he would be hurt to learn that some of his children and grandchildren experience feelings of being unwelcome in the house he built.

Pappy's House the way it looks at present

Pappy and Mammy's marriage produced 10 children in the twenty-six-year span 1933 – 1959.

The children are as follows:

Violet, born November 07, 1933
Irsiline, born February 13, 1938
Zelminica, born April 24, 1940
Carmelda, born June 11, 1942
Glendora, born July 27, 1944
Judith, born July 14, 1946
Orson, born March 24, 1950
Shirlene, born September 19, 1952
Patrick, born June 13, 1956
Nigel, born March 16, 1959

As at January 2022 in addition to the 10 children, his offspring grew to 32 grandchildren, 48 great grandchildren and 28 great great grandchildren.

Pappy's marriage to Mammy was a great one and it lasted for 58 years, from 1935 until he died in 1993.

Over the years, may people have told me several positive things about Pappy and Mammy. The following story affected me the most.

In 1980, this writer visited Carson Holder, a boy hood friend who lived at lower Mile and a Quarter with his grandmother Mrs. Olive Holder. Mrs. Holder was older than Pappy and knew him from the beginning of his marriage. They both attended The Bethany Christian Mission Church. Mrs. Holder told me with conviction and with a sense of awe in her presentation, a set of facts about Mammy and Pappy. She said, "You look around Mile and a Quarter and look at all the women who are married and their husbands do not go to church. What do you see? You see troubled and frayed marriages with the men causing all the problems and the women holding on because there was no other way. The relationships exist only by appearance. The reality is that they live in the same house but are as separated as if they were living in different houses. You look at Mammy and Pappy, and you see two model citizens, Pappy has never given Mammy those headache problems that the men in Mile and a Quarter give their wives". Many women in Mile and a Quarter have said it many times, openly and often, Mammy Waterman was fortunate to marry Pappy."

Pappy and Mammy on their 50th Anniversary

The marriage was a good one but the family also experienced pain. Some of the children caused their parents pain and embarrassment. What is admirable when these circumstances arose, is that Pappy and Mammy never forfeited their love for any of their children. This is evident with the fact that they never took drastic action on their disobedient children. They were outraged and expressed their disgust and surprise at the offending child. They counselled their children ending with the words "you ought to know better." However, the public could not openly tell that transgressions were committed and dealt with in his house. Pastor

Waterman kept his head high as he traversed the street. His quest to serve God superseded all the challenges he faced. He was unyielding in his mission to spread the gospel of Christ,

Remittances of funds is a global phenomenon. People migrating to larger countries for work, often remit some of their earnings to their families left behind. These funds in the first instance provide families with cash. In the middle to long term, when the money is spent, the country receiving the funds record and deposit these funds to their foreign reserves.

Pappy benefitted from remittances sent by his children. It started with his two oldest daughters Violet and Irsiline, and then a third daughter Judith. These daughters immigrated to England and remitted pounds on a regular basis to Pappy. The funds received; helped to buy food, clothing and other necessities for the family. In fact, these funds were important in helping to provide for the younger children left behind. In addition, about once a year, they combined to ship a parcel of household necessaries.

CHAPTER 6

A New Chapter in Life - The Bethany Christian Mission

The Bethany Christian Mission Church is located in a prime section of upper Mile and a Quarter St. Peter, Barbados. Established in 1938, it lies at the intersections of Rose Hill and Mile and a Quarter. For many generations, this section has been a commercial hub. It featured a supermarket, several rum shops and a gas station. Many people came to this section from surrounding areas for groceries, to buy gas, and to drink at the many watering holes found there.

Pappy attended this church from its inception. His devotion, sincerity and natural leadership skills led him to be elevated to the post of Deacon in 1942. In 1944, Pastor G. A. Ramsey led the church. The role of Pastor was part time, and Pastor Ramsey worked full time as manager of Jerusalem Agricultural Station. Owned by the Government of Barbados, the Jerusalem Agricultural Station researched the viability of fruits and vegetables for Barbadian soil types. It also grew and produced vegetables, and provided a husbandry service for domestic farm animals amongst other things.

Soon after Pastor Ramsey's installation at Bethany, there were whispered rumors that he was a member of a secret society or Lodge. Secret societies are organizations that conceal their inner functioning and membership. In 1944 Barbados, and even to this day, people view secret societies with suspicion. Secret societies inspire curiosity and distrust because of their masked nature.

In addition, because of their closed assemblies, some people view them as antichristian and/or even worshippers of evil. These views have led to many questions. Amongst the questions asked are, "can they serve the secret society and Christ at the same time? Can their service to Christ be at the leadership level?"

The following quotes from the King James Version of the Bible provide some answers and supports the thesis that you cannot serve Christ and the secret society at the same time.

1. You cannot serve two masters (Exodus 20, 3-6) - You should have no other Gods before me. You shall not make for yourself an idol. You should not bow down to them or worship them.
2. The Holy Bible is the only inspired word of God (2 Timothy 3: 16, 17) - This refutes the reading material of the secret societies.
3. Truth is the only thing to set men free, secrecy (bound by vows and oaths) is in direct conflict with the Holy Word (John 8: 31,32)
4. The brotherhood of secret oath bound societies, is incompatible with the fellowship of Christ's followers (1 John 1: 5-7)
5. The Bible forbids the followers of Christ from being unequally yoked with unbelievers (2 Corinthians 6, 14-16 – Ephesians 5, 7-17)

In 1946, Pastor Ramsey attended All Saints Anglican Church for a funeral. After the evening funeral and after socializing with friends he was late for a church service at the Bethany. The service had started and the congregation sang a hymn as they awaited his arrival. He hastily arrived at the church clutching his bag under his arm. As he approached the front pew, the bag fell, emptying its contents in plain view. The contents included a ceremonial fez, a ceremonial sash and a replica hatchet.

The song ended, an audible gasp engulfed the congregation, and then there was silence. He speedily gathered his regalia, and in a bundle returned them to the bag. The service continued, but a solemn reflective atmosphere pervaded amongst the congregation. A seemingly simple spill would move a whispering allegation to a loud and expressive conversation. The truth albeit inadvertently, was revealed for the congregation to see.

After the service was completed, a group of people stayed on to chat. The consensus arose that God had exposed the Pastor. Pappy spoke to the group, and amongst other statements said that you cannot serve more than one God. The group agreed that this issue was too serious to ignore. They were in unison that the Pastor violated their core beliefs. It is against this background that Pappy sprang to action and led an exit group of thirty people from the Bethany congregation.

Within two weeks of their departure, the group met and held a church service in the vacated home of Robert "Bob" O'Neal a once prominent Mile and a Quarter family. This service gave birth to the Mile and a Quarter Pentecostal House of Prayer. This meeting place served this new church for the next three years.

The people who followed Pappy were from the Mile and a Quarter area and surrounding districts. Included in the families who left to start the new church, were Mother Louise Blackman and her two daughters Ruth and Germaine Blackman, Carlotta Cumberbatch, Delly Headley, Winifred "Nanny" Benn and Leese Cumberbatch. These families would go on to be true pillars of the church, and their children, some unborn at the time of the exodus would continue the trend of active participants.

CHAPTER 7

Pappy's Vision and Purpose - Building the Church

T he Mile and a Quarter Pentecostal House of Prayer, or for some folk from the area "The Breakaway Church", moved to a permanent home at mid Mile and a Quarter in December,1948

The church bought the land from Mr. Bowen who occupied a small house on the land. Pappy walked to Ashton Hall, St Peter; a thirty-minute one-way journey to see Martin "Hand Lank" Ramsey. Also awaiting him was Peter Harris, an experienced mason. Pappy explained that the land was 50 feet wide and 100 feet long. He told Ramsey and Harris that he wanted the church built 30 feet wide and 60 feet long. Ramsey was a master mason with the ability to draw building plans. Prior to this meeting, Ramsey was informed, that he would be required to build this new church in Mile and a Quarter, and he had visited its location to see the out lay of the land. Pappy told him he wanted the building to look like all the other churches in St. Peter. In other words, he wanted a building of contemporary features. Ramsey drew as instructed.

The building would have a rectangular shape. It would sit East West with the east side where the road passes to be the main entrance. The building would have three doors; each would be

7 feet tall and 3 feet wide. Apart from the main entrance, there would be one door on the northern side and one at the southern side. There would be six windows, two windows on the North side of the building, two at the South side and two on the eastern or front of the building. The platform and altar would be located in the West of the building facing eastward. The congregation would sit on the eastern side of the altar facing west.

Pappy and members of the church worked assiduously to complete the project. The first phase of the project was to prepare the land. The land sat on a rocky elevation at the front and Pappy sought the skills of his brother-in-law to remove the rock face. Removing the rock made it easier to access the property. Joseph Bovell or Charlie Roach, as was his popular name, was the first of many volunteers on this project. He was married to Pappy's sister Irene; and it was his role to dynamite the front of the property.

Once the rock front of the land was eliminated, an army of females helped to remove the rock debris, storing it for future use. These women would go on to play a pivotal role in the overall construction project. They included the Blackmans, Roaches, Sugar Small and her daughter Stella, Marium Murphy a sister of Pappy, Carlotta "Baby Lot" Cumberbatch, Winifred "Nanny" Benn and Rhona Cumberbatch amongst many.

Samuel "Dicky Sam" Skeete was a plumber who worked for the Barbados Water Works Department and lived in the surrounding area. Pappy asked him if he could have a pipe connected to the main supply line in order to access water for the church's property. Sam Skeete promised to speak to his superiors at work. A week later, Sam reported to Pappy that his superiors approved the connection. The fees were quickly paid and in seven days, a water connection was made to the property.

This transaction was remarkable in the extreme because water connections often took up to six months to complete. Normally, a submitted application was a written one with an attached receipt of the paid fees. This application joined a waiting list until it reached the top. This list was lengthy and made so in part, by the slow nature of plumbers working on a particular project. In addition, plumbers moved in a leisurely manner from one job to another.

Pappy led the group that excavated the church's foundation. Young men from the area frequently came forward to help for intermittent periods. Charlie Roach employed choreographed dynamiting at the front to complete the foundation.

Buildings need concrete or clay blocks that are man- made, or blocks of stone that nature provides. Pappy needed blocks for the construction project and sought to procure some. Against the advice of his brother-in-law Eustace "Sonny" Murphy, reservations from his congregation, and people in the community, he approached Mr. DeCourcy Skeete the owner of Mt. Brevitor plantation and quarry. Mr. Skeete had a reputation in the community as a hard-nosed businessperson. He instituted stringent controls over his plantation operations in general and the quarry in particular. People that worked for him thought that he was a hard man with only an interest in profits.

Pappy awoke earlier than usual on the day he was to meet Mr. Skeete. It was a warm Saturday morning, and he brought the matter to God in prayer. He asked for strength, guidance, patience, wisdom, and for God to fill his mouth with the words to say. He asked that Mr. Skeete would recognize that this was a work of God. After talking to many people, he learned that Mr. Skeete had attended All Saints Anglican church, as a boy with his father. He was confident that building a church would appeal to his inner man. He was sure that Mr. Skeete would have retained in his heart some of the things he had heard whilst a boy at church.

Pappy approached him at his hilltop residence around 10.00 am. Mr. Skeete seemed surprised at the outset. He was probably thinking that a laborer was approaching for a conversation. Pappy told him he wanted to speak about the construction of a church at Mile and a Quarter. Mr. Skeete settled down from the anxiety that the surprise visit brought him. Pappy explained that he was building a church at Mile and a Quarter for the glory of God, and that he needed a donation of stone blocks for the project. After some contemplation, Mr. Skeete agreed to the request. He said, "Mr. Waterman, I can give you the chipped stones, you can take all that is required from the quarry." Pappy thanked him and wished him God's blessings.

Chipped stones did not fetch the prime rate in the market place; some stonemasons regarded these stones as defective. Despite the perceived defect, some stonemasons were able to cement the cracked portions and used them in the construction industry.

In the final analysis, Pappy's pitch was successful. It penetrated a perceived hard exterior and revealed a philanthropic heart. He gave thanks to God for the gift and for providing the words and the confidence to speak to Mr. Skeete. He thanked God for allowing Mr. Skeete to see God's hand in the project, and he asked God's blessings on Mr. Skeete.

Pappy hired Martin "Hand Lank" Ramsey as lead mason and Peter Harris an experience mason for the project. He met with them and asked if they could work with chipped stones. Given an affirmative answer, the work to get the stones on site started in earnest.

The following day, Pappy told his congregation that he was successful in acquiring the donation of stones. They rejoiced and thanked God for the gift. They saw the gift as bringing their dream of owning their own place of worship closer. They also asked God to bless Mr. Skeete.

Pappy's brother-in-law, Eustace "Sonny" Murphy was surprised at the success of acquiring the stones. He told Pappy he was "an action man, a man that could get things done." He offered to use his horse and cart to freight the stones from the quarry. For the twenty-five-minute journey, four stones per journey from Mt

Brevitor to Mile and a Quarter. The horse drawn cart went back and forth until there was a significant build up on the property. Pappy accompanied his brother-in-law on many trips to help with the loading and off-loading.

The project also needed sand, cement and lumber. Pappy employed the Brathwaite family to haul these materials. The Brathwaite family was a prominent business family in the Mile and a Quarter area, with trucking as one of their interests. Their son Lawson drove their truck; licence plate E105 to haul sand from Heywoods Estates.

The cement and lumber came from Plantations Limited a hardware store located at Speightstown. The truck did not have a dumping platform, nor were any of the materials loaded mechanically. To load and off load materials from the truck, the Brathwaite family employed Kelvin "Steel Heart" Jackman and Byron "Sugar Soil" Griffith, local men from the Mile and a Quarter area.

With the accumulating stones, and with the sand and cement in place, the masons initiated the building process starting with the excavated foundation. This was a community project; young men from areas near the church came to render assistance to the cause. In addition, the women who worked from the outset with the stone removal were present for this phase. Charlie Roach brought his dynamiting skills again to complete the front portion of the foundation excavation phase.

Soft stones are bulky and heavy building materials; stonemasons used them to establish the structure of the building. In order to place the stones in their places, young men from the area gathered to lift them in place. The taller the walls, the process of placing these stones became more complex.

The carpenters built a scaffold, adjusting its height as the building height grew. The masons employed a "rope and block" method to hoist the stones in place. Workers fastened a thick rope to a single stone and hoisted it on to a pulley. This pulley was located on the scaffold. The first task was to hoist the stones to the scaffold. To achieve this, there was the pull of those on the scaffold and a push from those on the ground. Once the stones were on the scaffold, workers maneuvered them into their places.

The masons made mortar by using a mixture of cement, sand and water to glue the stones to other stones and form a unified layer. Marl generated from the dynamited frontage, was added to the cement mixture to make concrete. This concrete filled the edges of the chipped stones and made them whole.

In 1948, Pleasant Hall plantation was a sugar cane estate with a quarry located on its land. Situated within a ten- minute walking distance from Mile and a Quarter, it employed some of the members of this new church. It is unclear how its owner Mr. A. H. Fields became aware of the church building project at Mile and a Quarter. He may have seen the building in progress in his travels, because Mile and a Quarter is the gateway to Pleasant Hall. However, one Saturday morning as the project was well on its way, his chauffeur stopped his car and walked up to the site. He asked to speak to Brother Waterman. Pappy emerged from the task of assisting the masons and listened intently as the chauffeur spoke. He said Mr. Fields wanted to donate some soft stones to the project. The offer was accepted and Pleasant Hall supplied stones. Installation of these stones took place in the upper levels of the building.

With the walls at their planned heights, the carpenters started the task of erecting the roof. The carpenters employed for this task were two relatives of Pappy, Cassie Waterman and Kenrick 'Nuggett' Harris who, in addition to their carpentry skills, were also joiners. Mr. Straker the expert joiner who lived next door would add to this combination and would contribute with his skill and experience.

The carpenters also used a pulley system to hoist the wooden beams to the roof. The workers tied to a rope, individual pieces of heavy wood, which they hoisted to the roof. The workers employed the same pulley system method in the hoisting of the soft stone. Once at the roof level, workers merged the wood to create the beam or spine that ran the length of the building. The workers then nailed the rafters to the beam and sloped them in a downward manner. These rafters were erected both left and right of the beam and were nailed to wood planted at the top of the sides of the building. On top of the rafters, carpenters nailed plywood sheeting to prepare for the erection of the roof. After laying the plywood, workers positioned the asphalt sheets to complete the roof.

After nailing the roof in its position, carpenters made and installed the thick wooden doors for both sides of the building and for the main front entrance. Ready to fit steel windows bought from Plantations Limited in Speightstown, were cemented into the building structure by the masons.

The masons erected the base of the platform at the western end of the building. The carpenters completed this phase of the building by erecting rails. The rails set the raised platform apart from the general assembly. The rails also created the altar where people would kneel in prayer.

With the roof, doors, windows and platform in place, it was time for the church benches. Whilst construction was in progress at the church, Pappy hired Benjamin 'Benjie' Arthur, a neighbor of the church and a carpenter/ joiner to construct the benches. The benches were eight feet long, and each seated a maximum of seven adults. The church accommodated thirty benches in its sanctuary.

With the construction completed, the church members painted the interior and exterior of the building. They painted the building white to highlight purity and to exemplify the birth of a new church. Many commented that the interior once painted seemed bigger than its actual size.

After the painting, an extensive cleaning of the church began. An army of church members, swept the floors, mopped and polished the interior. Church members then crossed the street to collect the benches from Benjamin Arthur's workshop. They walked them over, and equally laid them uniformly on both sides of the church building. An aisle of five feet separated the north from the south sides of the church. A distance of four and a half feet separated the walls from the benches to allow traffic between them.

With the church interior refreshed and furnished, members moved to the exterior to complete the clean up. They removed building debris from the property and loaded them on to Brathwaite's truck. They then removed the accumulating brush that had sprung up at the western end; now considered as the back of the church.

With construction and cleanup completed, the church received a wooden carving of the last supper of Christ. One Sunday morning before the church's dedication, Pappy accepted this gift. This carving was a gift from Mr. Frank Arthur, husband of Iretha 'Doll' Arthur a member of the church. Pappy had the carving placed on the back wall in the center of the platform. Mr. Frank Arthur emerged as a leader in the Mile and a Quarter community. His son Owen Arthur later became Barbados's fifth Prime Minister.

With the project completed, Pappy had won against the odds and many vocal opponents. Many in the Mile and a Quarter community had said that his congregation of thirty; mainly agricultural laborers, and led by an agricultural labor, could not generate the funds, nor were they sophisticated enough to purchase land and have a stone structure constructed.

Others said that he was too young to start and lead a church. By the completion of the church in 1948, Pappy was thirty-three years old.

Many had opined, that a man who lived in a wooden house, should not be expending that level of human capital in building a stone church. They believed the effort invested in the church, should have been invested in building a stone house for his family. His wife Mammy once told him there was much merit in those expressed sentiments.

Prior to 1948, and after that period, many ministries started and failed in their infancies. Many never got past the initial period of small gatherings to evolve into bigger congregations and construct a meeting place for their church. Some erected places of worship and the ministries went bankrupt. Given the significant failures that are prevalent in establishing churches, Pappy's success spoke volumes about his skills. It showed he possessed the leadership skills that enabled him to enjoy the confidence of his congregation. In addition, it showed that he exemplified, persuasive, negotiating and financial management skills.

When this writer was midway documenting Pappy's life, a friend sent me a philosophical thought. She sent it oblivious to my work on this project, and I believe that God had a hand in me receiving this message. It reads:

"God does not call the qualified. He qualifies the called."

This philosophical quote spoke directly to Pappy and his qualifications to start and erect a home for the church. His congregation would have seen some leadership qualifications. The community of folk outside the congregation could not see them because there was nothing tangible to see. However, God saw all the potential, and qualifications needed, and the leadership skills; and God enhanced them a thousand-fold.

In addition, the Bible laid down guidelines that guided his beliefs:

The LORD will make you the head, not the tail. If you pay attention to the commands of the LORD your God that I give you this day, and carefully follow them, you will always be at the top, never at the bottom. (Deuteronomy 28: 13)

With this in mind, we constantly pray for you, that our God may make you worthy of his calling, and that by his power he may bring to fruition your every desire for goodness and your every deed prompted by faith. We pray this so that the name of our Lord Jesus may be glorified in you, and you in him, according to the grace of our God and the Lord Jesus Christ (2 Thessalonians 1:11)

The Fitz Albert Waterman Memorial Church

CHAPTER 8

A Journey Fulfilled - The Dedication

With the building completed, it was time to dedicate the building. Pappy had met Pastor O Greaves as he then was, when Pappy was a Deacon at the Bethany. Pastor Greaves of Cleavers Hill, St Joseph had become his mentor, and had provided advice as he worked to establish the Mile and a Quarter Pentecostal House of Prayer. Pastor Greaves had introduced Pappy to the lawyer who would do the land conveyancing. He had also accompanied him to the lawyer when the conveyancing was completed.

When it was time, for the church's dedication, Pastor Greaves had been elevated to Bishop Greaves. Pappy invited him to preach at this special dedication service. He also invited the congregation at Cleavers Hill. Other Pastors and their congregations were invited. They included congregations from Checker Hall St Lucy, Six Mens, Roebuck, Moore Hill and French Village in St Peter, Bawden, St Andrew and the Garden, St James and other congregations.

Amongst those invited was Pastor Dobson, who was pastor of the Bethany church prior to J.A. Ramsey's tenure. He was instrumental in elevating Pappy to the role of Deacon. Highly respected amongst the congregation at the Bethany, Pastor

Dobson had remained neutral in the aftermath of the Pappy led withdrawal. Once he learned of the nature of the events at the Bethany, reports indicated that he said, "In the fullness of time, there will be clarity to these events."

On a warm Sunday afternoon in December 1948, The Mile and a Quarter Pentecostal House of Prayer was dedicated. The worship leader, Sister Carlotta Cumberbatch worked the congregation into a festive mood. She introduced well-known and popular choruses,

> *Send down the rain.*
> *Send down the rain.*
> *Send down the gospel rain.*
> *I want a revival in my soul.*

They sang lustily, clapped their hands in unison, stomped their feet, and danced to the rhythms of guitars and drums. At the end of each song, worshippers who were not already standing, stood to their feet and shouted at the top of their voices, "Hallelujah, thank you Jesus, Father in heaven send down your blessings."

When a choir appeared on the platform to sing, the congregation sang along.

> *Standing on the promises of Christ my King*
> *Through eternal ages, let his praises ring*
> *Glory in the highest, I will shout and sing*
> *Standing on the promises of God*
> *Standing, standing, standing on the promises of God,*
> *my Saviour*
> *Standing, standing, I'm standing on the promises*
> *of God*

It was now time for a soloist from the Cleavers Hill congregation.

I come to the garden alone
While the dew is still on the roses
And the voice I hear falling on my ear
The Son of God discloses
By the time she got to the chorus the whole church was
singing along
And he walks with me and he talks with me
And he tells me I am his own
And the joy we share as we tarry there
None other has ever known

When the song was finished, there were renewed shouts of Hallelujah, Hallelujah, thank you Jesus.

When the singing was over, or to use the term the church used, when song service was finished, Sister Cumberbatch said, "We are going to change the order of the service." As she spoke, she waited for the congregation to sit. Some members of the congregation were still on their feet dancing, praising God and exclaiming with passion how great God was. After everyone was seated and calm had come to the congregation, she spoke again.

"It is my great honor to introduce to you our spiritual leader Pastor Fitz Waterman." Pappy rose and made his way to the pulpit during acclamation and recurring shouts of praise God and hallelujah. With respect for his bowing head and hands that beckoned calm, silence returned to the sanctuary. He then addressed those assembled.

"Bishop Greaves, visiting Pastors and saints, today I stand before you humbled to welcome every one of you on this our special occasion. Truly, God has been good to us and has led us to this day. I can say without a doubt that we would not be here this evening were it not for God's grace. We asked God for guidance once we started on this journey, and he held our hands and brought us through. There were many in our district who doubted what we as a church could accomplish, but if God is for you, no man can stand in your way. In every step of the way, God has been with us. When we wanted to purchase land for this church, he provided this spot right in the heart of Mile and a Quarter. When we bought the land, God made the way smooth for us. When we wanted building materials, workers and volunteers, God showed up and directed us on acquiring them. I want you to know that we as a church never doubted that we would complete this project; we never lost sleep over how this project was progressing, because we knew that God was with us. God made our paths smooth and straightened every step we took, because we prayed and fasted through each development. Let me say how grateful I am to the members of this church. I am not going to call their names because I may forget one. They know who they are, and I salute them and thank them sincerely. The membership was committed to the cause, and they worked tirelessly for us to complete this church building. There was a fundamental solidarity of love and purpose. I must say that to be one in heart and mind is to be unified in every fiber of your being."

At the completion of this portion of the speech, prolonged and deafening applause engulfed the sanctuary. The congregation stood to their feet with some present clapping with their hands above their heads. Others were vociferous in their shouts of hallelujah and amen.

After motioning for the acclamations to cease, Pappy continued. "I am honored to host the assembled Pastors in our new home. I thank you and your congregations for coming and for your prayers and support over the past year. We ask for your continued prayers for we know that we can do nothing without God on our side, Amen."

When the speech was finished, there was a tremendous crescendo of applause; "Amen and God is good," filled the sanctuary. The bulk of the congregation sprang to their feet. The spirit moved Pappy to join in the acclamations. He raised his hands to the skies; his head leaned backward in an appellate posture to God. After waiting for the ovations to subside, the service moved on with Pappy inviting the visiting Pastors to speak.

Six pastors spoke that afternoon. They thanked God that another home was prepared for the propagation of Christ's teachings and principles. They prayed that God's words would penetrate to all who heard them. They also prayed that truth would reign. They all asked God to bless Pastor Waterman and the saints at the church. They assured all assembled, that Mile and a Quarter will be in their prayers, and that their churches were ready to provide assistance as needed.

Pastor Dobson prayed that the church would go on to touch lives in Mile and a Quarter and beyond. He said he could see God's hands working in everything he had seen about this church in the last four years. He said building a place to worship was a difficult undertaking and Pastor Waterman and the saints deserve much credit. He said there was no doubt that Christ's work must go onwards. He was confident that Christ's gospel will flow from the platform, and sinners would come to know Christ as their Lord and Saviour.

After the words of encouragement from the visiting pastors, Pappy returned to the rostrum to introduce the main speaker; now elevated Bishop O Greaves. He said Bishop Greaves had stayed by his side from the beginning of the church and throughout the building project. He said he gave advice with love, and with knowledge of church work earned over many years of pastoring and establishing congregations around the island. With great anticipation from the congregation, Pappy ushered Bishop Greaves to the rostrum with "Saints, I am honored and yet humbled to present to you a great servant of God, a man called to preach God's word and bring the sinner to Christ, Saints; I present Bishop O Greaves."

Bishop Greaves walked to the rostrum with the congregation on its feet. Someone in the congregation raised an impromptu song, and soon everyone was singing:

Satan you can't prevail.
Satan you can't prevail.
Because of disobedience
God cast you down from heaven.
All I want to know is the church is moving on.
Satan, Satan, Satan you can't prevail.

The congregation sang this song repeatedly. People were dancing, some had their hands raised in a worship posture, and others shouted hallelujah and thank you Jesus.

When this spontaneous celebration was completed, Bishop Greaves spoke.

"I am indeed honored to be asked to speak on this occasion. I met Pastor Waterman six years ago when he was Deacon Waterman, and since then, I have seen God working in his life. Pastor Waterman and the congregation here at the Mile and a Quarter Pentecostal House of Prayer deserve our congratulations for planting this house of God. Jeremiah 17:7-8 tells us:

"Blessed is the man who trusts in the LORD, whose trust is the LORD. He is like a tree planted by water, that sends out its roots by the stream, and does not fear when heat comes, for its leaves remain green, and is not anxious in the year of drought, for it does not cease to bear fruit."

At the end of this quote, there was spontaneous applause. Shouts of "Preach Bishop" and acclamations of "Hallelujah", and "Amen" filled the sanctuary. Some of the saints stood to their feet rejoicing in their praise and worship. The ovations abated, when the Bishop held out his hand to continue.

"I stand today on these premises to ask God to continue to make this house a place where the overseers of this house will always trust God. Where like a tree planted by the water, this church will forever bear fruit. That it will remain strong through the good times and the hard times. That its seeds will fall and spread everywhere and others will see its work and come to know

Jesus Christ as their Lord and Saviour. I pray that those who are lost in Christ, lost in this world of sin and shame, will come here and be as one with the one who seeks out the lost. I pray that God will mend the hearts of those who are broken. Those that are lonely and devoid of love will find warmth and fellowship here. I ask God that this house will be a light house for those in peril on the sea of sin and shame, not just in Mile and a Quarter but across the length and breadth of this island."

The Bishop's voice had risen to a crescendo and had descended to a whisper. He had spoken with passion and conviction and had come to a pause, a long pause. The congregation sprang to its feet again. This rise included the Pastors, who had been sitting on the platform responding gently to the move of the spirit in the church. They were now visually showing their appreciation for the words spoken by the Bishop. The applause and the boisterous affirmations of "hallelujah and praise God" went on unabated. The saints were dancing where they sat, but more so, in the main aisle of the church.

Hundreds of people on the outside of the building were craning their necks through the opened doors and windows. They were keen to see what was happening in the church. They were entranced with the joyous scene unfolding inside.

Bishop Greaves himself was rejoicing in the Lord with a jig, and with shoulders moving in a dancing motion. He had stopped and was now seeking the attention of the saints. He raised both hands in an outstretched posture in their direction. He beckoned calm so that he may complete his sermon. An elongated phase of worship waned at his gesture. He spoke again and silence ensued.

"I have had the privilege to speak to many dedication services, and I can say they are all different. I can tell you that the Holy Spirit is amongst us this evening. Saints, the Holy Spirit is moving in this place. It is moving here and moving there just like the day of Pentecost. The Holy Spirit has completely parked my prepared sermon and placed in my mouth the words that I have spoken here today. The Holy Spirit want us to worship God in spirit and in truth for these are the worshippers that God seeks out and blesses. The people of the world cannot accept him because they neither see him nor know him. Saints, I say to you, you know him, for he lives with you and will be in you. The spirit is amongst us because we are opening a door for sinners to come and see the light. A place for sinners to come to know him and experience his wonderful presence. We are placing here at Mile and a Quarter a storehouse of truth, and worship. A place set to spread God's word so that truth and faithfulness will prevail and the spirit of the Lord will come upon this place and engulf it with the power of a rushing river. So saints tonight we have a right to jump for joy, we have a right to praise God in the highest for we know that what we are doing is pleasing to God."

The Psalmist David tells us at Psalms 150:1-6:

Praise the LORD!
Praise God in his sanctuary.
Praise him in his mighty heavens!
Praise him for his mighty deeds.
Praise him according to his excellent greatness!
Praise him with trumpet sound.
Praise him with flute and harp!
Praise him with tambourine and dance.
Praise him with strings and pipe!
Praise him with sounding cymbals.
Praise him with loud clashing cymbals! ...
Let us praise him saints let us praise him.

The animated preacher spoke this Psalm, and his voice became louder and louder as the quote wore on. It seemed to be a call to arms by this General of Christ to the foot soldiers in attendance. He did not read when he quoted the Psalm. God had placed the words in his mouth, and he had delivered them with thunder. The other Pastors on the platform jump to their feet simultaneously as if it were a choreographed exercise. These senior soldiers of Christ heard the call and felt the weight of the call to arms. They exclaimed "Praise God, Praise God."

The congregation was also on its feet and were rejoicing in the Lord. They were proclaiming Praise God, Praise God. The musicians joined in and started playing the chorus Praise God. An up-tempo rhythm emerged, the musicians of guitarists and a drummer had seized the moment. People were stomping their feet, clapping and dancing to the rhythm:

> *Praise God, Praise God*
> *Praise him in the morning.*
> *Praise him at noontime.*
> *Praise God, Praise God*
> *Praise him till the sun go down.*

This spirited atmosphere went on for several minutes.

The electricity in the air at its zenith, reached a point of almost tangibility. Then it dissipated slowly, the musicians slowly faded the music out and the singing stopped. Several saints remained on their feet praising God.

The service had now moved into its third hour, and because the Holy Spirit filled the atmosphere, the passage of time went by unnoticed.

People on the outside spoke amongst themselves. They thought that the saints still dancing, albeit slowly in the church were in "the power". "She is in the power man," one man explained to another. Vehicular traffic passing through Mile and a Quarter did so at a crawl. Frustrated drivers frequently tooted their horns, as they tried to navigate their way through. The way through mid-Mile and a Quarter was made difficult by the cars that were parked both sides of the street. In addition, hundreds of people were on the roads and many were continuing to peer through the open doors and windows of the church.

Calm finally returned to the sanctuary, Bishop Greaves concluded his sermon with words of a prophetic nature. He said that this church at Mile and a Quarter would serve God's purpose well. I feel it in my inner being that this place of worship will be alight with the fire that comes with being close to God. I know that your spiritual leader Pastor Waterman is a man led by God. I feel it in my spirit that he will continue to lead you with that anointing that God has placed on him.

He invited the congregation to stand and invited Pappy to join him at the podium. He asked the congregation to stretch their hands towards him. Looking in the direction of the Pastors seated on the platform, he urged them to join him and lay hands on Pastor Waterman. He then removed a small vial of olive oil from beneath the rostrum and anointed his forehead. He then prayed:

"Father in heaven I bring your servant Pastor Waterman before you. Father, I ask you to anoint him with your holy spirit. I ask Lord that every time he comes to this rostrum to address the church that you will fill his mouth with the words to speak. I ask you to give him wisdom and understanding, I ask you to grant him discernment so that he will be able to interpret your words when you speak to him. Father, give him discernment so that he could see in this church when one of the flock is hurting or need some kind of assistance long before they even speak to him. Father God, fill him with love and compassion beyond measure so that his heart will be aligned with yours. Father, let love abide in this church, let fellowship flow through this church so that true brotherhood and sisterhood will reign forever. Father, I ask you to bless this Pastor in every aspect of his life, I pray that you will accompany him wherever he goes, Father let his daily living be an example for those around him and give him that presence that is shown when you are within us. I also ask blessings for this congregation at Mile and a Quarter Lord, we ask in your name Amen."

The church extolled a tremendous Amen in unison when the prayer was completed. They also sat and Bishop Greaves walked slowly back to his seat.

Pastor Waterman spoke again:

"Heavenly Father, we strongly feel that the lines of communication between you and us have opened wider on this special occasion. Father, we ask for your continued blessings for everything said and done this evening. We thank you for your servant who preached your word this evening, we thank you for all the other Pastors, and we thank you for the musicians and all those who gathered here to celebrate the opening of the home of the Mile and a Quarter Pentecostal House of Prayer. Father, as we start this new chapter, we ask for your hand to guide us through, Amen."

He then asked the congregation to stand. He said "Saints I am bringing this service to a close with the prayers that the Lord gave to Moses at Numbers Chapter 6: 24 - 26." He stood with his eyes closed, and with his hands outstretched to heaven. He then recited the prayer:

> *"The LORD bless you and keep you*
> *The LORD make his face to shine upon you and be*
> *gracious to you*
> *The LORD turn his face toward you and give you*
> *peace. Now and forever Amen*
> *Saints the church is dismissed."*

People filed out of the church, and some stayed back in the sanctuary to speak to familiar faces and to greet strangers. There was talk and laughter on the platform amongst the Pastors. Pastor Dobson embraced Pappy and there was chatter between the two men.

CHAPTER 9

The Commitment -
A New Beginning

The Mile and a Quarter Pentecostal House of Praise members formally moved into their house of worship, the day after the dedication of the church. When they moved to their new building, the officers of the church were as follows:

Pastor Waterman – Spiritual Head and Leader
Mother Springer – Superintendent
Carlotta Cumberbatch – Evangelist
Delli Headley – Evangelist
Winifred Benn – Missionary Leader
Ruth Blackman – Sunday school teacher

Pappy held a Monday night meeting and his faithful congregation attended in their numbers. Church services or sermons on nights were not as lengthy as those held on Sunday mornings. They were impactful nevertheless and saints went home filled with new information and inspired to hold on to their faith.

At the outset, there were thirty saints. As they moved into this new place of worship, the congregation had risen to forty adults and their children.

In their new home for this first Monday night service, the saints sang with gusto from the Melodies of Praise hymnal.

Would you be free from the burden of sin?
There is power in the blood, power in the blood
Would you o'er evil a victory win?
There is wonderful power in the blood

When the singing was over, Pappy preached the sermon. He said his message was on the topic Watch and Pray. Generally, when he preached during the week, he did not ask anyone to read a text from the Bible. He simply walked to the rostrum and spoke. He started by reminding them that as a congregation, they had advanced. He said the journey ahead would be as rocky and rough as when they first started. He said the challenges would not be the same, but there will be other challenges and obstacles to overcome. He reminded them that they had moved into their new home because of prayers and because they had trusted God. The congregation spurred him on as he propagated Christ's teachings. He urged that their prayers were to be unceasing. I say to you "watch and pray because we sit here tonight in this our new home because we watched and prayed." He said we must be vigilant in how we live for God. Satin will throw obstacles in our way, but we must pray and ask God for help and watch how he will bring you through. All problems and obstacles that stand in our way we will overcome them. In addition, if we pray for guidance, and if we listen to the voice of God, God will provide the guidance. We must watch and pray, Matthew 24:42 tells us to watch therefore, for we know not what hour your Lord will come. The Apostle Paul in a letter to the Colossians at 4:2 said we should devote ourselves to prayer, being watchful and thankful. We are reminded again at Matthew 25:13, to watch therefore, for ye know neither the day nor the hour when the Son of man cometh. Saints keep praying and keep watching for God has much more to reveal to us. He promises to provide more if we ask and if we watch and pray.

With the sermon completed, the congregation sang:

> Watch and pray that when the Master cometh
> If at morning, noon or night
> He may find a lamp in every window
> Trimmed and burning clear and bright.

When the singing ended, Pappy said a prayer for the church. He always started with these words:

> *How sweet the name of Jesus sounds*
> *In a believer's ear!*
> *It soothes his sorrows, heals his wounds*
> *And drives away his fear.*
> *It makes the wounded spirit whole*
> *And calms the troubled breast;*
> *'Tis manna to the hungry soul,*
> *And to the weary, rest.*

Then he prayed:

"Father in heaven we come before you to thank you for providing us a place of our own. Father, we ask that you place a ring of protection around this place when we are not here and when we are here. Father, we place our trust in you because we know that you can make the impossible happen. Father your word tells us that you raised Lazarus from the dead. We ask you to hold our hand and lead us forward and give us protection as we set out to secure new souls for your kingdom. Father, we ask you to place in our hearts the desire to pray, the desire to call on you all of the time. Place in our hearts Lord a desire to serve you, a desire to be close to you. Father as we close this service, we ask you to take us home safely, we ask that you protect us from any accidents along the way. Hear our prayer oh Lord, Amen."

When the prayer was completed, Pappy dismissed the church with the Doxology:

> *Praise God from whom all blessings flow*
> *Praise Him, all creatures here below*
> *Praise Him above the Heavenly host*
> *Praise Father, Son and Holy Ghost*
> *Amen, Amen,*

Once the church had its own place to worship, Pappy aligned his church with membership with a group of churches that included, French Village, Six Mens, Moore Hill and Speightstown. These churches were all located in the parish of St. Peter. He also aligned the church to those from other parishes.

The headquarters for the churches he sought alignment with, was located at The Grange, Passage Road, St Michael. The leader of this group was Bishop Taitt, a Barbadian who resided in New York, USA. Bishop Taitt also pastored a church in Harlem, New York and its membership were mainly Barbadians.

The organization did not have a constitution or a manual that spoke to the roles of the churches or individuals. It did not possess an administrative structure. It was a fragile leadership structure. Following the Bishop were two Superintendents that completed the leadership group. The Superintendents were Edmund Skeete and Leonard Cumberbatch. They both resided in Barbados and they both came from the northern Parishes of St Peter and St Andrew respectively. The Superintendents presided over baby dedications, marriages, and funerals at the various churches. In addition, the Superintendents made regular visits to the churches in the organization to preach and to maintain a presence. They also attended to listen to any issues the pastors or membership wanted to discuss. The Superintendents were largely unpaid, but the status and respect that came with the roles were substantial.

Superintendent Skeete was a familiar presence at Mile and a Quarter. He was popular amongst the membership and his preaching was always thought provoking. He became a friend and confidant of Pappy and often attended his house for non- business reasons.

The churches gathered once yearly at The Grange for what was called Quarterly. Bishop Taitt would be present at this meeting. Quarterly was a lengthy church service, with the various churches providing reports on their programs, membership and the amount of money collected for the Quarterly meeting. Churches earned plaques and other memorabilia for a variety of achievements. These achievements included the church with the greatest congregation, and the one that collected and presented the highest offering.

Bishop Taitt preached at Quarterly services. Dressed in a Bishop's robe, he and his attire commanded attention. Whereas the Superintendents and Pastors wore business suits, Bishop Taitt wore vestments synonymous with his office. He wore a white robe adorned with a red tunic and a black sash that came around his neck and stretched to his knees. He preached at the Quarterly services and his deliveries were animated and persuasive. His sermons were lengthy and when he finished; sweat pored profusely.

Bishop Taitt died in 1981 and in his final will and testament; he designated The Grange to his immediate blood relatives. When this information reached Pappy, he immediately spoke to Superintendent Skeete. He said that willing the church to family members showed that the gathering for Quarterly services was a business enterprise. He said bequeathing The Grange to the church organization would have been a decision to benefit the organization. This would have allowed the church union to carry on and even expand with more churches. He said he was removing his church from the group and would not be attending any other services at The Grange. Pappy removed his church from the organization and the other churches followed. Firstly, those from the north of the island and afterward, other churches across the island.

Bishop Taitt's legacy remains today for reasons not directly related to the church groupings. As Bishop, he sent barrels of food and clothing from America to individuals and some churches. Mile and a Quarter Pentecostal did not benefit from any of this largesse.

In addition, Bishop Taitt recruited several young people from churches in the church groupings to immigrate to the USA. Several young people and some established with homes and families from Pappy's church took the plunge and moved to the USA. Those leaving included people that played significant roles in the church. The sheer number of people who left including some key personnel were detrimental to the church at Mile and a Quarter. Despite the losses, the church was still able to move on. New people arrived and filled the gaps created with the losses.

People immigrating to the USA initially moved to the city and state of New York. Upon arrival, they were mainly undocumented and found comfort amongst the Barbadian population that resided there. Most significantly, they attended Taitt's church in Harlem, New York. Sunday morning worship in Harlem was a reunion for many of the past saints from Mile and a Quarter, but also saints from other churches across Barbados. Many spoke fondly of their time at Mile and a Quarter and the family and friends they left behind.

With the benefit of hindsight, the net result of Taitt's action has led to a compelling conclusion. He reduced the membership of churches in Barbados with his immigration scheme and increased membership at his church in New York. Direct influence and cash flow generated more authority, than indirect influence and cash flow.

Pappy and most of the original congregation of the church were young people. Some of these saints were newly married and were either starting or completing families. Sister Winifred Benn's son Haynesley was born in January 1949. Christened on February 20, 1949; he was the first child to be christened at The Mile and a Quarter Pentecostal House of Prayer. Pappy's son, Orson was born in March 1950 and was the first of his children to be christened at the new church in May 1950. Since the church's inception, it has performed christening ceremonies mainly for members or relatives of those that attended. However, others in its vicinity have had their babies christened at the church.

Over the ensuing years, many people from the Mile and a Quarter area attended the church, including children and young adults. Many of them went on to respectable positions in many employment spheres. There were pastors and evangelists, teachers, community leaders and lawyers. There was a government minister and a diplomat. There were politicians and a Prime Minister. There were businesspeople, senior civil servants and a bank executive. Here are two of note:

Owen Arthur is the son of Iretha 'Doll' Arthur. He would go on to be an Economist in the Barbados Ministry of Finance, and a Lecturer at the University of the West Indies. He became a Member of Parliament representing the Parish of St. Peter from November 22, 1984, to March 06, 2018, and Leader of the Opposition in Parliament from August 1, 1993 to September 06, 1994 and October 23, 2010 to February 21, 2013. He served as Prime Minister from September 06, 1994, to January 15, 2008. To date, he is the longest serving Prime Minister of Barbados. He died on July 27, 2020.

Haynesley Benn, the son of Winifred "Nanny" Benn was the first child to enter into holy baptism in the church in February

1949. He would go on to be a primary school teacher in 1967 and started the first 4H club in St Peter in 1969. This club would progress to dominate the various awards of the annual 4H Achievement Day. He would become General Manager of the Barbados Agricultural Society, the island's main agricultural cooperative; he served this organization from 1975 - 1997. He also served in the private sector as a Business Executive for the Barbados Shipping and Trading Company Limited, a Barbados business conglomerate. He contested a seat for the Barbados Parliament and served in the Barbados Senate from 2008 - 2013. He also served in the Cabinet of the Government of Barbados as Minister of Agriculture from 2008 - 2010, and Minister of Commerce and Trade from 2010 - 2013. He joined the Diplomatic Corp serving as Consul General of Barbados at Toronto, Canada from 2013 - 2018.

Owen Arthur

Haynesley Benn

CHAPTER 10

Church as it Happened

There were services every night of the week at the Mile and a Quarter Pentecostal House of Prayer. They were as follows:

Monday – General Service.
Tuesday – Bible Study.
Wednesday – General Service
Thursday – Prayer Meeting
Friday – Young people service
Saturday – Concerts, plays and other presentations
Sunday – Corporate Service

Sunday morning service was the main service of the church. It was truly a special day, and the church designated the day as "Lord's Day." On Sundays, everyone in attendance dressed in their finest clothes, their "Sunday Best." Reverence and solemnity pervaded the atmosphere of the church on this day. One Sunday morning when I was in my early teens, I attempted to read The Barbados Advocate newspaper in the church. As soon as I opened it, Evangelist Carlotta Cumberbatch came up to me and said quite forcefully that I could not read the paper in church.

Sunday service started at 11.00 am but before the service, Sunday school for children started at 10.00 am. The first Sunday school Superintendent was Mother Springer. The first teacher in the new building was Sister Ruth Blackman. Another Sunday school teacher was Sis Carlotta Cumberbatch. Sister Frida Griffith followed and afterward, Sister Pat Gill. Sister Gill started as a Sunday school teacher and served from 1969 – 1983. Promoted to Superintendent in 1975, during her tenure, she revolutionized several practices that were in place before she started. She kept meticulous records of the children attendance records and their offerings. These offerings paid the bus fares for the children, at the church's annual excursion. In cases where there were surpluses, the offerings also covered other family members. For several years under her tutelage there was an increase in attendance and surpluses of funds after the annual excursion. After she was married, she became Sister Pat Eastman and moved to the Eastern Parish of St. Phillip with her husband.

On Sunday mornings, the church sang from the "Joy and Gladness" hymn book. The service started with a senior member of the church "leading song service". Leading song service meant leading the congregation in morning worship. The member chose the songs that were sung, and therefore, had the capacity to control the tempo of the service. It was common for the member leading the song service to recite the lyrics of the song in introducing it to the congregation. The leader's comments went as follows:

> *Redeem how I love to proclaim it.*
> *Redeem by the blood of the lamb.*
> *Redeem through his infinite mercy.*
> *His child and forever I am.*

Saints, we are redeemed by the blood of the lamb; we are redeemed through his infinite mercy. For these reasons, we have a right to jump and sing. Please turn to page nine in your hymnal and let us lift our voices and play our ten string instruments to the glory of God.

Song service on Sunday mornings lasted for about forty- five minutes. After worship, the leader announced; "I will now change the order of the service." She then invited a soloist to sing or a member to give a testimony or invited a visitor to speak if he or she wished to do so.

The worship leader then introduced Pastor Waterman to the rostrum. The introduction was not formal or glorifying. The worship leader simply said, "I am going to change the order of the service;" and invited Pastor Waterman to the rostrum. She then exited the platform. After the exit, Pappy walked to the rostrum and started with a greeting to the church.

"Saints I greet you in the name of Jesus our Lord and Savior. It is an honor to be in the house of the Lord, and to give thanks for the many blessings he has bestowed on us. It is a privilege to stand before you and proclaim the matchless name of Jesus."

Pastor Waterman then announced the many events ongoing in the church. He mentioned those who were sick and needed prayer, and included the time he would be leading a delegation to visit the following Saturday. He then told the church of the many invitations received from other churches. He asked if the saints were interested in attending these services. Responding with a negative was quite rare. With positive responses received, he placed the invitations as he completed them, in his jacket pocket. He would later ask one of his daughters to reply on his behalf.

Next was the sermon. He announced the topic, asked someone usually a young member to read the Bible text that supported his thesis, and then proceeded to preach. It is generally believed that he showed up unprepared to preach and once he started, the anointing of the Holy Spirit filled him and he spoke eloquently for about forty- five minutes. This is true in some cases, but he did not necessarily show up cold. He had a topic in mind and spent the night praying and meditating on the topic. In the early years, there were times when he prepared the night before with his older daughters. He told them the topic he wanted to speak to, told them where the references were in the Bible and he prepared in that manner.

On receiving church invitations, the night before the announcements, a family member read the invitations to him. He then recalled them verbatim and made the announcements. Every Sunday morning before church started, various church leaders met and briefed him on the activities of their departments. With this information memorized, he was able to tell the congregation of the progress of the various programs.

When Pappy spoke, his voice commanded attention. Smooth and clear, and conducive to public speaking, his voice was a gift from God. This is a re-enactment of a sermon by Pappy in 1978. You will notice that he pointed to a person to read a passage of the Bible for him. This practice took place only at his home church on Sunday mornings. When he was away from his home church, he announced the topic and spoke about the topic with pertinent Bible references.

This writer recalls this sermon as presented to his church on a Sunday morning in June 1978.

"Today, I am going to speak to you on the topic of love. The text will be taken from 1Corinthians, Chapter 13. Those with Bibles in the congregation, please turn to the text." As the congregation turned the pages of the Bible, he speaks again. "I am going to ask Sister Pat Gill to read this text for the benefit of us all." Sister Pat stood, read the text and sat again. Then the sermon began.

"This is the Apostle Paul writing to the church at Corinth in reply to the question, what is love. In answering that question, the Apostle laid down a road map for us to follow as it relates to love. He tells us that we are nothing if we do not love. It does not matter if you are active in church, it does not matter that your tithe is accurate and on time, it does not matter if you can speak in tongues. It does not matter if you have enough faith to move mountains. If you do not love, you are nothing and unworthy in the eyes of God. You cannot truly serve God if you do not love. You must love yourself, your neighbor and work colleagues. Saints, you must demonstrate love in your daily living. You must visit those that are sick and hurting and provide comfort to them in their time of need. You must comfort those that are grieving and provide a shoulder for them to lean on.

You must extend your hand and help someone along the way. These acts are pleasing to God and are demonstrations of love. When you work together to lessen the load for everyone else working on the job, that is love and it is pleasing to God.

The Gospel of Matthew 5: 44 and 45 tells us that we must love our enemies and pray for those who persecute us, that we may be children of our Father in heaven. Did you hear clearly, what was said in that text? The advice given is that we are to love those who say bad things about us. Those who abuse you and do all manner of evil things to you. You may ask how is it possible for me to love someone who say bad things about me. How can I love someone who abuses me? You can; what you should do is to dislike the hurtful words and the hurtful actions but love the person who spoke those words or perform those actions. Love with all your heart the person whose actions caused you pain.

I will now speak in particular of God's love, 1 John 4:16 informs us that "we have come to know and have believed the love which God has for us; God is love, and the one who abides in love abides in God, and God abides in him."

When you have the love of God in you, it comes out of you in a spontaneous manner. It is a love that shows that caring side of you. It is involved with the needs of others and not of self. Remember that with God in you, you will give your all to others without seeking compensation or favor in any way. With God's love in you, it does not matter if the person you are extending love to deserves it. With God's love in you, you will not reserve it only for a select few. God's love is an all-encompassing, always present, selfless love shown towards everyone. God's love is greater than that of a father or a mother and we all know of the strength of a mother's love. It is greater than I love you and all of your faults. God's love allows you to love without recognizing the faults. It allows you to see the whole, faults, or no faults.

God's love is so great for us his children that he sent his only begotten son so that all of us believers shall have everlasting life. John 3:16 expresses this love in its basic and yet pure way. It follows then that when God calls us to worship, he calls us to love him the way he loves us. Saints show love to the world around you, let God's love direct your actions and he will brighten your path.

I now speak to our young people on the issue of love as it relates to marriage. The Apostle Paul tells us at one Corinthians 7: 8-9 that it was better to marry than to burn with passion. The Apostle was referring to burning for passion for the opposite sex. To marry you must find a partner. How a partner looks is important but must not be the main decision to respond to a proposal to start a relationship. Your partner needs not be six feet tall and be a household name for a sport. What your partner possesses must not be the main factor in starting a relationship. In every decision, in every serious thought you make with regards to love, pray about it.

Start by finding someone who believes and honor God the way you do. Second Corinthians 6: 14 tell us, do not be yoked together with unbelievers. For what do righteousness and wickedness have in common? Put another way, what fellowship can light have with darkness? If you look around you, in this very community, the consequences of unequally yoked relationships are abundantly clear. I promise you that you will feel better, and your love will grow if you have your husband or wife beside you as you worship God. I have had Mammy by my side at every meeting and everywhere I went, and I can say without hesitation, our love has grown. I was married when I was twenty years old, and my marriage is still strong today because she is at my side for every event I attend. Finally, be wise when you choose, look as far into the future as possible and imagine what you want and where you want to be. Remember, always ask God for guidance, to show you the path, and be there with you when you choose.

I close with these final thoughts to you; scholars call these words of philosophy. Love in all its forms will always bring us together. Love will always demonstrate its truths. Amidst every eventuality, it will always see us through, amen saints."

He then asked the congregation to stand, he started to sing and soon everyone was singing:

> *Love lifted me.*
> *Love lifted me.*
> *When nothing else could help*
> *Love lifted me.*

Before the song was completed, many people had gathered at the altar waiting for prayer. Before he left the rostrum, he reminded the church that the altar was open for prayer. Then he told the congregation, that there was room at the cross for everyone. Those words prompted the church to sing again.

A senior member of the church raised the song, and the church sang again in harmony.

> *There is room at the cross for you*
> *There is room at the cross for you*
> *Though millions have come, there's still room for one*
> *Yes, there's room at the cross for you.*

With singing in motion, he summoned seniors in the church to the altar. The response came from seniors such as Evangelist Cumberbatch and Mother Benn. These seniors and Pappy prayed individually with the kneeling saints.

On the occasional Sunday morning, the church dismissed themselves. This occurred in cases where the altar was brimming with people needing prayer. Everyone in attendance knew it was over when all those kneeling at the altar had their prayer needs met. People simply drifted away to chat or wait for a loved one, the formal proceeding simply petered out.

CHAPTER 11

Revival Services at Home and Away

At Home

Revival services were also called "The two Weeks of Services" at the Mile and a Quarter Pentecostal House of Prayer. This was a highly anticipated event. Every second week in the month of November, the church held these services. In preparation, the church prayed and fasted for a week. The main aim of revival services was to see people come to know Jesus Christ as their Lord and Savior. In addition, these services were there for the Holy Ghost to come and fill the members. When the Holy Ghost has poured into individuals, those around will see and hear the speaking of tongues. This is a manifestation of the presence of the Holy Spirit

Revival services brought a hive of activity to the church. Every night, the congregations of other churches filled the Mile and a Quarter Pentecostal church. Associated churches were each designated a night, and their pastor preached the gospel that night. Every night, people on the outside grabbed every vantage point to see what was going on in the church. Every night, large volumes of cars and people clogged the streets of Mile and a Quarter.

The services started with the song service led by a senior member of the church. The services were lively, and those in attendance both local and visiting, sang at the top of their lungs and danced to the music.

> *The Lord's our rock in him we hide*
> *A shelter in the time of storm*
> *Secure whatever ill betide*
> *A shelter in the time of storm*

At the end of each song, there were shouts of "Hallelujah" and "Praise God" from the congregants. It is at the praise and worship stage that some church members would "get in the power." This meant that the anointing of the Holy Spirit was "upon you." People who were in the power shook and fell to the ground. When people fell, senior church members such as Evangelists or Deacons came to their assistance and prayed with them. The aim of the prayers was many fold. One reason was to hear if they were quietly speaking in tongues, and if they were interpretations of the spoken language. Some congregants spoke quietly and some loudly when the anointing of the Holy Spirit came upon them.

In cases, where the language spoken in tongues was audible, there were people who interpreted the words spoken. Another reason senior church members prayed with someone who may be lying was to wake the congregant up. This allowed the member to partake further in the service if it was just a momentary spiritual intervention. Another reason was to give comfort and support to the person filled with the Holy Ghost. Some members in the power stayed on their feet, dancing, and praising God. When this occurred, to maintain order, the congregation waited until the member had completed their experience.

After the singing and the falling in power were completed, the preacher spoke. Preachers who spoke at revival services seemed to speak with more authority. Their words seemed more power filled. Many have said that because the presence of God was in the room, those who had his anointing spoke as if anointed. This writer heard Pastor Ifill, referred to as Mother Ifill from the Hillaby Church in the Parish of St. Andrew. When she spoke, her sermon was so power filled, if felt thunderous as she presented it. Her words were fluent, she moved her head from side to side and the congregation was silent, even transfixed as this woman of God poured out what God had placed in her heart.

I have also witnessed preachers who had responses from the congregation with each sentence spoken. Chants of "Praise the Lord", or "Preach Pastor" or shouts of "Amen" filled the air as they spoke. These preachers were animated and filled with the Holy Spirit. They did not refer to notes or their Bibles as they spoke.

It was customary that after the preaching, people would line up to get to the altar. Where there was no altar call and there was a line to the altar, Pastors and other senior church members prayed with individuals. Long lines to the altar satisfied the reason for the services. Those not from the immediate vicinity were urged to choose a church near to their homes. Pastors reminded them to start anew and to "make their calling and election for Christ's kingdom sure."

At other times, there were altar calls. This was a specialty amongst Pastors. The greatest exponent of altar calls was Pastor Vera Cumberbatch. She was Pastor of the Six Mens Pentecostal House of Prayer in the Parish of St. Peter. She spoke with a soft voice and constantly reminded those present of the urgency of accepting Jesus Christ in their lives. She created an atmosphere of solemnity. There was complete silence when she spoke; she stressed the need for those present to lay their sins at the altar and accept Christ before it was too late. She would leave the platform and walk to the back of the church speaking in tongues as she walked. It was a slow walk. When she walked, it seemed she was walking by faith because she walked with closed eyes. She would stop by some of the pews in the aisles as she walked. With her hands held aloft in a prayer's position, she would utter words to those in the pew. After her comments, some folk sitting in the pews where she stopped would walk to the altar. Many walked in a weak manner to the altar. They were unsteady on their feet. It was a mesmerising sight.

When she walked back to the platform, the altar overflowed with people from within and out of the building. Another Pastor would start a song.

> *Softly and tenderly, Jesus is calling*
> *Calling for you and for me*
> *See on the portals He's waiting and watching*
> *Watching for you and for me.*
> *Come home, come home*
> *Ye who are weary come home*
> *Earnestly, tenderly Jesus is calling*
> *Calling, "O sinner come home."*

At the outset of the singing, Pastor Cumberbatch sat in her seat on the platform. Throughout the singing, she sat quietly, and with closed eyes. Her head tilted toward the heavens, with folded palms in a prayer position. These hands appeared to provide support to the Pastor who in that moment seemed oblivious to her surroundings.

Meanwhile, there were long lines of people advancing to the altar. As the advancement progressed, the congregation sang additional songs that appealed to the heart. The song "Search me oh God", which lyrics were adapted from Psalms139: 23 – 24 was particularly moving and drew introspection from those in the congregation.

> *Search me, O God, and know my heart today*
> *Try me, O Savior, know my thoughts, I pray*
> *See if there be some wicked way in me*

Cleanse me from every sin, and set me free.
Lord, take my life, and make it wholly Thine
Fill my poor heart with Thy great love divine
Take all my will, my passion, self and pride
I now surrender, Lord, in me abide.

By the time this song was completed, Pastor Cumberbatch was awake to her surroundings and responsibilities, and took the lead again. She invited all that could hear her voice to examine themselves. She repeatedly asked if everyone knew what God would find, should God search his or her heart. Her question sought to immerse all those that were able to hear her voice. To those looking in from the outside she pointedly referenced the fact that God saw them and was appealing to their souls. Her pleadings would cause souls to come in from the outside.

With the altar filled and overflowing into the aisles, the Pastor invoked a single prayer for the gathered throng. Those needing individual prayer were asked to stay back to have their needs met. It took several minutes before the altar was cleared of those leaving.

Pappy then closed the night service with a prayer of blessings for the proceedings and all gathered. He thanked God for coming into their midst, and for allowing his spirit to bring the lost ones into his kingdom. He asked God for travelling mercies for those who came from far. He ended as per tradition with a powerful and beautiful recitation of Numbers 6: 24 – 26

> *The LORD bless you*
> *and keep you*
> *the LORD make his face to shine upon you*
> *and be gracious to you;*
> *the LORD turn his face toward you*
> *and give you peace.*
> And he would add *"now and forever amen."*

Revival at Other Churches

Invitations frequently arrived for Pappy to preach at revival services at other churches. In almost every case, he and the church accepted those invitations. In the 1950's – 1970's the church was transported to the revival services in what Barbadians called pickups. Pickups were vans/trucks that during the day, freighted goods for customers. If an opportunity arose to transport people, the owners would fasten benches to the vehicles and transform them into people moving vehicles. Unlike buses, these vehicles were loaded from the back.

Brother Cornelius "Corny" Waterman was a member of the Mile and a Quarter Pentecostal House of Prayer, and he owned a pickup truck. The church employed Brother Corny to transport the congregation to revival services.

People oftentimes asked if Brother Corny was a relative of Pastor Waterman. The two men did not practise a blood family relationship. Their relationship was one based on the brothers in Christ principle. However, Brother Corny grandmother and Pappy's grandmother were sisters. The women were both born in French Village, St Peter. Pappy's grandmother migrated to Mile and a Quarter, whereas Corny's grandmother spent all of her years in French Village. Today, French Village remains a bastion of the Waterman family descendants.

Whenever the church travelled for revival services, the pickup was always fully loaded. Pappy sat at the back of the vehicle, and when they reached their destinations, he was the first to disembark. Like a general leading his army, Pappy led his church members into the church.

They filed in to the pews and he headed to the platform to sit amongst the resident and visiting Pastors.

The services followed the general pattern of up-tempo gospel songs for praise and worship. The reason for using these songs was to generate the atmosphere that invited the Holy Spirit into the midst of the church's service. These songs moved the congregation into a fever pitch mood. These songs made it conducive for saints to experience the presence of the Holy Ghost. Many saints experienced the presence and the power of the Holy Spirit. Some spoke in tongues. For others, the scene was a reminder of the day of Pentecost when the spirit of the Holy Ghost came and transformed the upper room where Jesus's disciples were gathered. The singing and dancing went on for about forty- five minutes or longer. Ultimately, the length of the singing, dancing and joyful celebrations, depended on "how the Spirit moved."

After song service, the church prepared for the ministering of the word. With spirits high, and the congregation buzzing with expectation, Pastor Williams invited Pappy to speak. The resident Pastor's introduction followed a prominent pattern within the Pentecostal movement when it came to Pappy.

"Saints of God, tonight we welcome the man of God from Mile and a Quarter. He has won souls for Christ across the length and breadth of this island. People love to hear him because God has anointed him to speak his word. God places on his heart the exact words to say to his people when he is ministering. Saints his faith is solid, it is firm like a tree planted by the waters. Saints if you have any doubt about your faith, if Satan has been tempting you, if you have problems that have you burdened; I encourage you to listen to the man of God, Pastor Waterman. Throughout the years, his ministry has been one of encouragement. He has taught of overcoming difficulties; his life experience is overcoming difficulties. God has anointed him with the skills to speak to problems and to command Satan to get out of the lives of God's people. Saints I present to you Pastor Waterman."

The sermon presented here is a re-enactment of a sermon given at Moore Hill Pentecostal church at Moore Hill, St. Peter in 1980. This writer witnessed the actions of the congregation and the events as recorded are accurate.

Pastor Waterman rose and moved to the lectern with great adoration emanating from the congregation. Pastors in attendance and the congregation were standing. Shouts of hallelujah and praise God rang out. Some in the congregation were clapping and some were stomping their feet. The folks looking on from the outside huddle closer in anticipation. Their craning necks penetrated the windows and the doors. During the acclaim inside, the western side of the church started singing a song. Many young people populated this side of the church. The song rose in a crescendo as it roared like a wildfire through the upbeat congregation. The song was catchy and people swayed from left to right to the natural rhythm of the song.

> *I got shoes.*
> *You got shoes.*
> *All God's children got shoes.*
> *When I get to heaven, I'm gonna put on my shoes*
> *I'm gonna walk all over God's heaven,*
> *Heaven, heaven*
> *I'm gonna walk all over God's heaven.*

Everyone was now standing as the entire audience became engrossed with the spirit of the moment. Hands were clapping, tambourines were playing, and the mood of heavenly merriment reverberated in the church. During this jubilation, Pappy swayed with his clasped hands held high, from left to right to the natural rhythm of the song.

The process faded out after about fifteen minutes with shouts of "praise God, hallelujah and we must give God the glory." The singing stopped and most in the congregation returned to their seats to await the next phase of the service. However, a young woman was still dancing. Surrounded and held by three older women, she skipped and danced, and her movements took her left and then right again. She went forward in a bowing motion and then straightened up. She spoke repetitively, "in the name of Jesus, in the name of Jesus."

A fourth woman joined the older women providing support for the young woman filled with the spirit of the Holy Ghost. Lady number four had a large white sheet in her hands. After ten minutes, the chants of the young woman became softer. Her eyes remained closed, and her movements remained jerky. She fell backward and the older women held her and guided her gently to the floor of the church in a seated and then lying position. Once in the lying position, the young woman was covered with the sheet by one of the older women. All four of the older women sat around and kept watch.

The rest of the congregation remained quiet and they all seemed patient throughout the movement of the spirit within the young woman. Pappy stood at the lectern; he keenly surveyed the proceedings. Now it was his time to preach.

"Saints of God of this beautiful church here at Moore Hill, I bring you greetings from the saints of Mile and a Quarter. It is always great to come to Moore Hill and share Christ's gospel with the saints here. Every time I come to Moore Hill, the spirit of the Lord fills this place with fire from heaven. This tells me that Moore Hill is a praying church; it tells me that the saints here have truly accepted Christ as their Lord and Savior. It tells me that the saints here are truly saved. I can sense that they are sanctified and filled with the Holy Spirit.

Tonight, my sermon is about faith, I am here to bolster your faith, but also to get those who need to be faithful, those who need to trust God more, to do so. For those looking on from the outside, I want you to know that faith in God can set you free from your sins. The sin of alcoholism, the sin of dishonesty, the sin of fornication. I want you to know that faith in God can move mountains and calm the raging seas. You may ask what faith is. Hebrews 11:1: tells us that faith is the assurance of things hoped for and the conviction of things not seen. So how do you make that statement easier to understand? I answer that question and say to you, it is being sure of what we hope for, and certain of what we do not see. It is knowing that God has heard your prayer, it is knowing that he will answer that prayer.

Faith is central in our walk with God. The Bible tells us that faith is belief in the one, true God without actually seeing him. So, it is fair to say that without faith you would not be here tonight, without faith you would not hold the beliefs deep in your heart that someday you will be going home to be with the Lord. Saints, faith sustains us when we are down, faith sustains us when our backs are to the wall, and faith sustains us when there is no way or no one to turn to for help. Without faith in God, we are not able to reconcile the fact that he understands. Without faith in God, we will not have the confidence to believe that he will make a way for us. Without faith in God many of us will simply despair and despise everything around us when there is sorrow.

Saints, people without faith have nothing to hold on to when they have problems. People without faith when they are troubled are like boats drifting in the vast ocean. They drift at the mercy of the wind and the waves. They are unable to chart a course because there is no rudder beneath them that will allow them to steer their vessel. Saints, tonight we have a rudder, we can chart a course, and we have something, on which we can hold. We have faith that God will bring us through, we have faith that God will remove every mountain that stands in our way. We have faith that God will carry us through every valley of life and bring us to a place of comfort and rest. We have faith that God will make every crooked path straight. Saints tonight I urge you to hold on to God unchanging hand, I urge you to be unwavering in your faith until the master comes."

Throughout the sermon, congregants were often on their feet shouting, "Preach Pastor, praise God, hallelujah." On many occasions, Pappy had to pause to allow the saints to express themselves. One woman also started the song:

Faith in God can move a mighty mountain.
Faith in God can calm the sea.

The song did not sparkle, and; no fires burned that crackled through the congregation and as a result, it quickly faded. Although the song faded, the woman remained standing waving a maroon flag, back and forth. She stopped singing but started yelling "faith in God, faith in God." An elder of the church at Moore Hill, who obviously knew this woman, in a very calm manner, and with a smile on his face, beckoned her to sit with his calming hand gesture. She returned the smile and sat, and Pappy resumed his sermon.

"Saints tonight I am going to tell you a story, a story of faith. Before I start the story, I want you to know these things. You cannot buy faith or transfer it to another person. You cannot give it to your children. Every one of us must exercise our own faith. We must strengthen our faith by pray and supplication, we must allow our faith to grow by growing deeper in our beliefs in God. You nurture your faith when you come to church and hear the word of God. You nurture your faith by gaining knowledge of faith in action. This story is an example of faith in action.

In Chicago, a man lived with his wife and four daughters. He was a wealthy man, and he was a believer. He was an elder in the Presbyterian Church. One summer his wife and four daughters set out on a trip to England. He was not with them because of pressing business reasons. On the way to England, their ship collided with another larger ship and went to the bottom of the ocean. All four of this man's daughters were lost when the ship went down, but his wife survived. Do you know what he did, he did not despair, he held on to his faith, he held out to God and wrote a song that spoke of his faith".

When peace, like a river, attendeth my way
When sorrows like sea billows roll;

> *Whatever my lot, Thou hast taught me to say,*
> *It is well it is well with my soul.*

Pappy recited the first verse, but by the time he got around to the chorus, the congregation started to sing.

> *It is well (it is well)*
> *with my soul (with my soul),*
> *It is well, it is well with my soul.*

The church sang the chorus twice, and towards the end of its second rendition, the platform announced that the song was at page 225 of the hymnbook. Those with hymnals in the seat pouch before them, hurriedly found the hymn and the congregation sang the second verse.

> *Though Satan should buffet, though trials should come*
> *Let this blest assurance control,*
> *That Christ hath regarded my helpless estate,*
> *And hath shed His own blood for my soul.*

"Saints that is an example of faith in God, this is an example of faith in action. This man had God and faith in God on which to hold. His faith was tested and he stayed faithful. He could have asked God why he brought this sorrow on his household. He could have said God I trusted you and you let me down in my time of need. He did not cry pity me, instead; he said it was well with his soul. Instead of cursing God, he thanked him for sending Christ to shed his blood for his soul."

"Saints, if faced with adversity tonight, will your faith sustain you to the point that you could say, with all sincerity; it is well with your soul? Saints, if you were at your lowest ebb, will your faith remain intact despite the severe issues that have plagued you? The songwriter asked, will, your anchor hold in the storm of life.

The anchor he wrote of; is your faith. Will it hold in the storm of life? That is a question, which you must be able to answer with confidence. I beseech you saints to get closer to God. The closer you are to God, the more faith you will have, and the greater the will to carry on though Satan should buffet."

Pappy paused to wipe his sweating brow. Before the break, the congregation was in rapt attention as he told the story of Horatio Spafford. Silence permeated the church. The profound context of the message and the probing questions that flowed from the sermon contributed to this state of affairs. In addition, the tragedy that unfolded before the song and the deep emotions that the song elicited were also contributors to this atmosphere. This silence is also present on the outside of the church. Since the sermon started, those on the outside had remained welded to their positions.

Pappy had experienced these moments many times in his ministry. God had given him this gift to reach out and touch people with his words and beautiful voice. He is clearly in his element. The anointing of God is upon him. Pappy is physically in the room, but he is a mere instrument for the words of God that flowed through him. This anointing had taken him to a place beyond the four walls of this church. There was a glow on his face as he preached. I had seen a glow before this night but did not understand what it meant. It appeared to me that on this night the glow seemed brighter. Was I the only one to see this glow around Pappy's face? I asked my mother if she had noticed. I did not get a direct response, she said "Son, he; is doing God's work." I wanted more, I thought she would elaborate but she kept all the information that she had witnessed over the years to herself.

Pappy spoke again. He did not restart the sermon. He urged all those who needed to have their faith restored or strengthened to come to the altar. There was a rush to the altar, so he changed his instructions. He asked those who needed prayer to stand where they presently were. To those on the outside he instructed them to come in and stand in the corridors.

With these new instructions, the entire congregation in the small church was on its feet. The corridors were impassable, and there was pressure from those outside who were longing to get inside. Pappy urged those trying to get inside to stay calm. He reminded them that God saw them and could reach them where they were. He then instructed all those who heard the sound of his voice to stretch their hands towards the platform. The audience responded and he began to pray.

He started with his favourite starting point,

> *How sweet the name of Jesus sounds*
> *In a believer's ear!*
> *It soothes his sorrows, heals his wounds,*
> *And drives away his fear.*
> *It makes the wounded spirit whole*
> *And calms the troubled breast*
> *'Tis manna to the hungry soul*
> *And to the weary, rest.*

"Father in heaven, you came down to earth to save us and you told us to have faith in you, you told us to trust your word. You said that if we have faith as much as a grain of mustard seed, we can say to the mountains go, throw yourself into the sea, and it will be done. Father in heaven, as we gather here at Moore Hill, I am reminded that you have also said that righteous men will live by faith. Father, I ask that you mold us in your image, and make us people of righteousness and faith. I ask Lord that you will fill our hearts with faith, that you will fill our minds and souls with faith in you.

Father, we ask that you guide our actions so that we can live by faith and have a life that is wholly committed to you. A life where our faith in you will be transcendent so that others would see our life, recognize your presence in our lives, and come to know you. Father, I ask that you cleanse our thoughts of impurities; we ask that you allow us to keep our eyes fixed on you and you alone! Father, give us the strength, the knowledge, and the will to keep our eyes steadfast on you and your word, so that we can live lives righteous in your sight.

Father, for those bowing before you for the first time, I ask that you save their souls tonight. I ask that you bring them to your throne of mercy where they will find acceptance and love. Father, touch them in a meaningful way tonight, and cleanse their sins so that they may start anew in you, Amen."

After the prayer, Pappy moved gingerly to his seat on the platform. The other Pastors on the platform applauded him. After sermons, it was normal for him to be tired and in need of fluids and rest. Once seated, he drank a glass of cool water. With the sermon completed, and with the fluids consumed, he appeared recharged. The glow around his head was gone, he seemed normal again, handsome, and professional.

Pastor Williams the resident Pastor moved to the lectern. He thanked Pastor Waterman, a man of God, for bringing a message of significance once again to the saints at Moore Hill. With the congregation remaining on their feet, he told them that they had heard the word of God. He told them that we now know without any doubt that without faith in our lives, we are helpless. He said he was closing the service, and if anyone had a specific prayer need, they should stay after the service. He then started singing the Doxology:

> *Praise God from whom all blessings flow*
> *Praise Him all creatures here below*
> *Praise Him above ye heavenly hosts*
> *Praise Father, Son, and Holy Ghost*

When the song was finished, Pastor Williams wished everyone good night and God speed to those that were travelling. He said a closing prayer:

"Father in heaven, we thank you for the excellent service that we have had tonight. Father, help us to practise what we have been taught, may our faith be restored or strengthened. Father, help us to become like Christ and bear more fruit for your kingdom. Father, grant us faith, and provide it to us for our daily living. Father, let everything we do be in line with your word. Father be with us as we leave this place, protect us as we travel to our places of abode, and grant us peace in our hearts and contentment in our souls. In Jesus' name, we pray, Amen".

The congregation filed out of the church, but Mammy stayed on waiting for her beloved Pappy. Pappy was busy speaking to other Pastors on the platform. When the conversations concluded, Pappy moved towards the exit, with his wife by his side. Other Pastors remained to pray for those waiting for individual prayer. Brother Corny Waterman moved his vehicle up the hill with some difficulty because of the crowd. He was aiming to be closer to the church's entrance. This was to facilitate Pappy, his wife, and the other saints from Mile and a Quarter. Once loaded up, Pappy asked if everyone was onboard. With a positive reply, he signaled the pickup to move on home. Another revival service was completed, Pappy had preached God's word, and everyone went home to await the next service.

CHAPTER 12

The service of Harvest Thanksgiving

The modern British tradition of celebrating Harvest Thanks Giving in churches in the autumn began in 1843. The Reverend Robert Hawker invited parishioners to a special thanksgiving service at his church in Cornwall. The hymn "We plough the fields and scatter" became a regular hymn for these services and that tradition continued in Barbados. In Barbados, the service was adapted to suit the completion of the sugar cane harvest. To that end, every April, churches across the island conducted this service.

The Harvest Thanksgiving service was an important item on the Mile and a Quarter Church's calendar. This service marked the end of the sugar cane harvest. In addition, it also served as a major fundraiser for church operations. It took place on the last Sunday afternoon in the month of April. The saints especially the children looked forward to this service.

Decorations infused the church with a festive mood for this service. In the early years, the membership decorated the church with flowers embedded in coconut palms. These coconut palms were strategically arched and placed around the altar and the doors. In addition, a variety of fruit and vegetables, some placed at the altar and some used in decoration, added to the festive atmosphere in the sanctuary.

For at least six weeks before the service, Sunday school teachers prepared the children for the event. The children received Christian poetry or philosophical thoughts to learn and recite on the day of the service. Rigorous practice followed until the day of the service.

The church choir was also activated for the Thanksgiving Service. The church employed an itinerant choir director and his associate to prepare the choir for the big day. George Roach as Choir Director and Elridge "Lil Man" Benn his assistant intensely rehearsed the choir into perfection. In addition to directing the choir, Roach sang bass. His assistant Benn sang tenor.

The service always started with the hymn "We plough the fields and scatter" This song seemed to set the tone for the evening proceedings.

We plough the fields and scatter the good seed on the land, but it is fed and watered by God's almighty hand:

> *you send the snow in winter,*
> *the warmth to swell the grain,*
> *the breezes and the sunshine,*
> *and soft refreshing rain.*
> *All good gifts around us*
> *are sent from heaven above*
> *we thank you, Lord, we thank you,*
> *Lord for all your love.*

After brief remarks by Pappy, he introduced The Master of Ceremonies, and the programme began in earnest. The Master of Ceremony would call each child to the platform where the children recited poetry to the audience. Rapturous applause followed for those who completed their recitations. For children that failed, an applause also followed when rescued from the platform by the Sunday school teacher or a family member.

On the day of the service, the choir with its blended voices sounded like an organ. Roach's bass anchored the smooth sound that resonated. When it was the choir's time to perform, crowds outside of the church jostled for every vantage point.

One song that was sung yearly and was a favourite with the congregation was "Echoes from the Burning Bush":

> *Moses stood on holy ground,*
> *Fire from God descended down,*
> *Set the roadside bush on fire – (Bush on fire)*
> *Then the Lord did there explain,*
> *Through His servant should remain,*
> *All the echoes from the bush on fire – (The bush on fire)*
> *Oh I can hear the echoes from the burning bush,*
> *How they thrill my soul – (How they thrill my soul)*
> *Oh I can hear those thrilling echoes from the burning bush,*
> *Point me to the goal – (Point me to the goal)*

After the choir completed this song, in its southern gospel style, rapturous applause and shouts of approval filled the atmosphere. The four-part harmonies, the repeats "how they thrill my soul," all combined to present a rendition that appealed to those in attendance.

At the end of the service, the church sold the fruit and vegetables that stood in the sanctuary. Church members, whether visiting or regular, or folk who stayed on the outside to observe, all came forward to make a purchase. The proceeds of the sale went to the coffers of the church.

Towards the end of the 1970's, the church abandoned the adornments and the abundance of fruit and vegetables at the altar. The church directed its members to sell the produce they normally brought and bring the cash to the service. The practice of bringing cash eliminated the perennial sight of having large quantities of produce at the church after the service was completed.

CHAPTER 13

Church Excursions

Every August, the church held an excursion. These excursions were primarily for the Sunday school children; but adults also attended. Pappy looked forward to the excursions because he saw it as a reward for the children. Two days before the excursion, families baked a variety of cakes. On the night before, other meals were prepared. Macaroni pie, rice and peas, baked chicken and a variety of sandwiches were prepared for the outing. Packed neatly in a variety of containers, and placed in large baskets or boxes, the food was ready for transportation. A bus from the government owned Transport Board was hired and the church made the hour- long drive to the King George V memorial park. Pappy and Mammy always sat at the front of the bus. On the way to the park, church members sang songs and played their tambourines. Some bus drivers became involved with the beautiful music emanating in the bus. They nodded their heads, tapped the staring wheels with their left hands, all in time with the rhythm of the beat.

> *A little more oil in my lamp to keep it burning.*
> *A little more oil in my lamp I pray.*
> *A little more oil in my lamp to keep it burning.*
> *Keep it burning till the break of day.*

When the church arrived at the park, families moved to benches, or under large trees for the shade. They spread large plastic covers on the ground and dished out the meals to their children. After the meals, the children played, frequently going back for more food. Then it was time for the church to gather, sing and play in the park's gazebo.

The church gathered in the gazebo to sing and have fellowship. This gathering brought other churches that were associated with Mile and a Quarter. These churches included Farm Road and French village Pentecostals of St Peter, and Hillaby Pentecostal, in St Andrew. They would sing, heartedly playing their tambourines and clapping their hands to the glory of God.

> *Satan you can't prevail.*
> *Satan you can't prevail.*
> *Because of disobedience, God cast you down from Heaven.*
> *Satan you got to know, that the Church is moving on.*
> *Satan, Satan, Satan you can't prevail.*

Pappy spoke lightheartedly at these fellowship sessions. The following speech is a re-enactment of a speech made in August 1978.

"I want to give thanks to God for bringing us safely to this park another year. I am grateful that his mercies endure forever. I am glad that we are in our right minds, and because of that, we have a right to sing God's praises. We are here to celebrate our children, we want them to know that we are aware that they are the future, and they will be the ones to carry on Christ's work. The boys and girls of today will be the men and women of tomorrow. We know that when we old ones are gone; these children will step up to win souls for Christ.

I want to congratulate the Sunday School Superintendents and their assistants who are here with us today. I applaud you for your service in preparing our children for the Kingdom of God. I pray that God will bless you as you continue in your ministries. I specifically would like to thank my Superintendent at Mile and a Quarter, Sister Pat Gill and her assistant Sister Aldeane Jordan. You have done a great job with our kids and I was told that the children look forward to your classes on Sunday mornings. We thank God for raising these two up to serve with distinction. I will not tarry any further, I know you all want to continue to play and have fun. Please bow your heads, Father in heaven we thank you for our Sunday school children; we thank you for bringing us all here to celebrate another year. We ask your continued blessings, amen."

Those gathered sang again before dispersing to play and eat more food.

> *When we all get to heaven*
> *What a day of rejoicing that will be,*
> *When we all see Jesus*
> *We will sing and shout the victory*

The excursion bus left the park about 4.45 pm to get to Mile and a Quarter before the sun went down at 6.00 pm. On the way back, there was more singing, the playing of tambourines and the clapping of hands. Small children slept most of the way home. They were tired after a day of playing in the park, also, the heat of the bus made it conducive to sleep. Sometimes the bus would drive slowly past the island's airport, and everyone would just peer through the windows to admire it. On the way home, the bus drove slowly and quickly as the driver assessed the time left for arrival time. As the bus drew closer to Mile and a Quarter, the song that signalled the end broke out in the back. This song was different from all the songs previously heard in the bus. A small group embraced the song; they were mainly teenagers. They sang:

Why, why my money gone.
Went to the park and now get home.
Why, why my money gone.

When the bus finally reached the church, people disembarked the bus with their much lighter bags and boxes. They headed home happy that another excursion had come and gone without incident.

CHAPTER 14

Spiritual Experiences

T hey were many spiritual experiences that family members and others encountered after Pappy's death and burial. However, before Pappy died, he travelled to England in 1983 with a painful knee injury that made walking difficult. In fact, he sought assistance to walk to the plane and to deplane. Two days after arriving in England, he attended a church service. During the course of the service, the pain disappeared from his knee. He felt a warm feeling around the knee, and when he stood to understand what the feeling meant, he was able to place his full weight on his knee, pain free. This enabled him to join in the dancing and merriment that was very much in session.

In addition, in December 1993, on the last day at his church and before the day's sermon, the church had noticed that he was in a buoyant mood. Prior to this day, no one could recall this level of buoyancy. He danced to most of the songs sung that day. He was vociferous in his adoration of God and his goodness, and he urged the church to show more sincerity to God when worshipping in song. He also presided over the dedication of new metal windows for the building. After the dedication and the service of songs, he rose to preach the sermon. Pappy preached his final sermon ten days before he died. During the sermon, he said these words to his congregation at Mile and a Quarter Pentecostal.

"I have done my best; I have done what God wanted me to do. He is ready to call me home. I have built this church, if you do not maintain it; it will be a matter for you and God. I have run my course; I am going home to be with the Lord. At my funeral do not cry for me, have no concerns whatsoever about me. You must rejoice; my funeral service must be one of joy and gladness because my calling and election to God's kingdom has been assured."

After the church service was completed, church members also noticed, that he was hugging church members with a big happy smile on his face. This was uncharacteristic of him, prior to this day. He also greeted church members with a handshake, and in some cases, this followed with his left hand on their shoulders.

In April 1992, Pappy's daughter Irsiline who lived in the city of Boston, USA visited him at his home in Maynard's Road. Retired from work, she spent two months with him. On the day of her return in June 1992, he told her "The next time you are back you will not see me, I have a feeling that I will be soon going home." He died January 1993.

A year after Pappy's death in March 1994, Zelminica his daughter reported that he appeared to her. She had been ordained as Pastor of the Mile and a Quarter Pentecostal House of Prayer. In an audible voice one early morning, he urged her to take the role of Pastor seriously and work diligently for the master.

In November 1998, this writer visited Barbados to spend some time with an ailing Mammy. At about 4.30 pm on a hot sunny day, I was resting in the bedroom adjacent to where Mammy was laying. Family members called the bedroom where Mammy laid the family bedroom. It is the place where Mammy and Pappy slept. As a boy when I felt ill, I headed for the family bedroom. Laying in the family bed was like a balm in Gilead, it brought me comfort and relief.

As I half slept on that warm sunny day, I felt a very warm hand on my leg. This hand startled me, and I arose in a screaming panic to see a disappearing shadow. My sister Glen, who was visiting from America, heard my scream and ran into the bedroom to investigate. I told her I was resting when I felt a warm hand on my leg. I told her that it startled me, and I awoke to see a disappearing shadow. She opined that Pappy was there to heal my feet and I had scared him off with my scream.

Soon after Pappy died, his daughter Irsiline said he appeared in a dream to her one early morning. He was dressed in white and in a very audible voice, he said, "stop crying, your work on earth is not done, you have to stay and finish God's work." He then proceeded down a tunnel that was well lit and disappeared.

Another moment was in December 1999 when Mammie was ill. His daughters Irsiline and Zelminica were in the bedroom where she laid. They reported that Pappy appeared in the bedroom and with an audible voice said, "Do not worry; I am taking her home with me."

When Irsiline's husband Johnny was ill, in October 2006, he laid in bed, and Irsiline sat at the head of the bed. Whilst sitting, she reported that Pappy appeared and stood at the foot of the bed. He said something that Irsiline could not decipher, and then he waved goodbye and disappeared. A year later, Johnathan died whilst sitting at the foot of the bed. He was at the same place Pappy stood at the foot of the bed.

CHAPTER 15

Services of Thanksgiving for the lives of Pappy and Mammy - So shall it be in the End

Pappy

Pappy passed away on January 31, 1993 at his home following a stroke. Days before, he had fallen ill and hospitalized at the Queen Elizabeth Hospital, Barbados's main hospital. After three days in hospital, he requested a discharge. He asked to be returned home to allow him to "die in my own home." It was a sad day for his family but those who were hurting were soon comforted when reminded that he said they should be rejoicing.

Pappy's passing brought his scattered family together again. His children, grandchildren, nephews, nieces and other family members all hurriedly flew to Barbados for the funeral. They came from various parts of England, America and Canada. Family members living in Barbados met and ferried them from the Grantley Adams Airport first to Maynard's Road, and then on to other accommodations.

On February 08, 1993, his body laid for public viewing at his beloved Mile and a Quarter Pentecostal House of Prayer. His family, both blood and church, Pastors, Evangelists and members of the community where he lived and served, gathered for this his last service on earth. The church overflowed with those paying their last respects, and the windows and doors filled with onlookers. Although it would normally be a solemn occasion, the service planners deviated from mournful songs to joyful ones. This was in keeping with his wishes; they sang:

> *Sing the wondrous love of Jesus*
> *sing His mercy and His grace*
> *in the mansions bright and blessed*
> *He'll prepare for us a place.*
> *When we all get to heaven*
> *what a day of rejoicing that will be*
> *When we all see Jesus,*
> *we'll sing and shout the victory.*

A beautiful solo rendition of "How Great Thou Art" brought tremendous applause, shouts of Hallelujah and thank you Lord, from the congregation. Pastors spoke about working with him and his ability to see the bigger picture. Some said his sermons were thought provoking, and others said they left them inspired. One Pastor said what would always stay with him "is the anointing that poured forth when he was preaching God's word."

His daughters, Zelminica, and Irsiline read two Bible lessons before the sermon.

His nephew Pastor Carl Murphy preached a sermon entitled "Laying down your life for the glory of God." He chose the Bible verses John 15:13-14 and said he was reading from the King James Version. He urged the church to read it aloud with him. The congregation loudly read "Greater love has no one than this, that someone lay down his life for his friends. You are my friends if you do what I command you."

He said Pappy's friends were the people he served, his neighbors and his community. He applauded him for setting aside his own interests for those of others. He said we should emulate Pappy, by putting aside our wants and allocate our time, and talents for the benefit of others. He said if you serve those around you, as commanded by God you will become God's friend, and you will be awarded the fruits of being his friend.

In the midst of the service, this author delivered the eulogy:

"Good afternoon, we are gathered here to give thanks to God for the life of Fitz Albert Waterman. My father always gave God thanks for everything in his life. In good times and in bad times, he thought God was in control. Therefore, it is fitting that we call this service a Thanksgiving Service.

My father was born to Mary Anne Waterman and Samuel Walker on January 06, 1915. He married my mother Myrtle Jestine Waterman on August 11, 1935. The union produced ten children. They are Violet, Irsiline, Zelminica, Glendora, Carmelda, Judith, Neta, Orson, Patrick and me Nigel. As vowed before God and the church, they remained married until the event that brought us all here today to celebrate his life.

In the ensuing years of raising children and pastoring this church, all and sundry affectionately called him Pappy. I was once asked where the name Pappy came from. I could not answer the question directly. Instead, I said it meant beloved father, revered dad.

The name Pappy resonated love, honesty and integrity. It reflected a man with a kind heart. Pappy loved his children dearly and cared deeply about his church family. He agonized over issues his children faced, and the problems individuals in his church family were encountering.

Pappy commanded respect from his neighbors and others he encountered in his daily living. Folk saw something distinctive about him, something special about his manner as he went about his living. It was the presence of God in his life. God's light radiated through him, and it came shining through, especially when he preached.

Many of you know Pastor Waterman for his work as spiritual leader of this church. He branched out from another church in this area and played a monumental role in having this church built and consecrated in 1948. His branching out was a manifestation of his integrity. Integrity was his mantra back then and it sustained him for the rest of his life. Pappy served unchallenged as Pastor of this church since 1944. The 49 years he spent leading this church, is an indicator of the respect he garnered not only as a spiritual leader, but also as an individual.

Pappy's greatest legacy may be his leadership with distinction of this church. His commitment to the cause of Christ through his leadership of this church was unwavering. One can also add that an abiding legacy would be the way he lived his life, and his unremitting service to God. Yesterday, I saw a former member of this church. He informed me that the way Pappy lived his life created a lasting legacy that would influence generations to come. He argued; "if you influence one generation, chances are they will instill those values in their children and this process will continue for many generations."

As my dad, I had the honor to listen to his advice on many occasions. I can tell you with the benefit of hindsight, he was right most of the time. His painful early life story, and the way his life evolved, inspired me to aspire for higher learning. I will be spreading the value of higher education to my children."

After the Thanksgiving Service, the funeral procession moved slowly to St Peter's Parish Cemetery, for the interment. Once in the cemetery the body was carried directly to the graveside. The Anglican Priest the Reverend Mark Harewood, conducted the graveside service. After words of condolences to the family, he said he had gotten to know Pastor Waterman and enjoyed talking to him. He described Pappy as a man of God, and a man who possessed a stirring intellect. He said he was a true neighbor who welcomed him to the neighborhood. After the kind words, he said this prayer reading from the Anglican Book of Common Prayers.

"Almighty God, with whom do live the spirits of those who depart in the Lord, and with whom the souls of the faithful are in joy and felicity. We praise and magnify your holy name for all your servants who have finished their course and kept the faith; and committing our brother Pastor Waterman to your gracious keeping, we pray that, together with him and with all those who are departed in the true faith of your holy name. We may have our perfect consummation and bliss, both in body and soul, in your eternal and everlasting glory, through Jesus Christ our Lord. Amen. We therefore commit this body to the ground, earth to earth, ashes to ashes, dust to dust; in sure and certain hope of the resurrection to eternal life."

As the grave preparers closed the grave, the assembled saints sang the hymn, "And Can it be" with reverence:

> *And can it be that I should gain*
> *An interest in the Savior's blood?*
> *Died He for me, who caused His pain—*
> *For me, who Him to death pursued?*
> *Amazing love! How can it be,*
> *That Thou, my God, should've died for me?*
> Refrain
> *Amazing love! How can it be,*
> *That Thou, my God, should've die for me?*

Pappy's sojourn on earth was over once lowered into the grave. His family wanted the internment at All Saints Anglican Church, but this request was denied. Historically, All Saints Church served as the burial place for the people in its surrounding areas. The people in the area had an emotional connection to the church for several reasons. The greatest connection came from the fact that everyone attended All Saints Schools. In addition, it was convenient, but also a tradition for the people of Mile and a

Quarter to walk to the church to pay their final respects to love ones and neighbors.

At the time of Pappy's death, All Saints Church was enforcing a policy of burying only members of the church. For about five years preceding his passing, at times, this policy was enforced. At other times, the policy was not enforced. An examination of this policy revealed it to be a whimsical ploy. This policy was implemented to appease some arrogant and ignorant congregants. They thought that even in death; All Saints Church should only serve their interests. If they knew the church's history, they would have realized that they were repeating it.

On the day of Pappy's funeral as we escorted his body out of the church, a childhood friend came to speak with me. He had noticed that the cortege was facing toward the St. Peter Cemetery and away from All Saints Church. He did not offer any words of condolences, nor did he comment on the service or the prevailing atmosphere. In an insensitive act, he proclaimed quite forcefully that All Saints Church belong to its members and only its members should be buried there. As a member of the choir, he had given himself the authority to speak for All Saints church burial policy.

As I laid in bed the night of his funeral, I reflected on his life. It became quite apparent that Pappy suffered at the hands of All Saints. In the beginning at its school, and at the end its Church.

Mammy

Mammy died on July 26, 1999, following a lengthy illness. Her passing brought her scattered family together again. Her children, grandchildren, and other family members all hurriedly flew to Barbados for the funeral. As with Pappy, they had come from various parts of England, America and Canada. Family members living in Barbados, again met and ferried them from the Grantley

Adams Airport, first to Maynard's Road, and then on to other accommodations.

Her funeral services took place on August 05, 1999. The first service was at Mile and a Quarter Pentecostal Church and the second service at All Saints Anglican Church. The officiating minister at Mile and a Quarter was Pastor T.N Walcott. The Reverend Stephen Thorne officiated at All Saints Anglican Church. Her daughter Judith Nicholls, and granddaughter Debra Worrell read the first and second Bible lesson respectively at Mile and a Quarter, and her granddaughter Pastor Dr. Verlyn Waterman– Taylor delivered the homily at All Saints.

At Mile and a Quarter, the church choir sang to a rousing applause the hymn "Each step I take":

> *Each step I take my Saviour goes before me,*
> *And with His loving hand He leads the way,*
> *And with each breath I whisper "I adore Thee;"*
> *Oh, what joy to walk with Him each day.*
> *Each step I take I know that He will guide me;*
> *To higher ground He ever leads me on.*
> *Until someday the last step will be taken.*
> *Each step I take just leads me closer home.*

Her family members selected and gathered on the platform to sing the song "Is this not the land of Beulah". It was one of Mammy's favorite hymns and the congregation was alerted to this fact. The audience was invited to sing along, and everyone sang with reverence.

> *I am dwelling on the mountain,*
> *Where the golden sunlight gleams*
> *O'er a land whose wondrous beauty*
> *Far exceeds my fondest dreams;*
> *Where the air is pure, ethereal,*

Laden with the breath of flowers,
They are blooming by the fountain,
'Neath the amaranthine bowers.

Is not this the land of Beulah? Blessed,
blessed land of light, Where the flowers
bloom forever, And the sun is always
bright!

After the family hymn was completed, Pastor T.N. Walcott invited this author to read the eulogy.

"Good afternoon, we are gathered here today to give thanks to God as we commemorate the life of Myrtle Jestine Waterman. My mother always gave God thanks whether it was something we ordinary folk thought was something good or bad.

My mother was born to Ruth Anne Richards and Nathan 'Moses' Cadogan on July 02, 1915. She met and married my dad the late Pastor Fitz Albert Waterman on August 11, 1935. As vowed before God and the church, the union remained until death took her beloved husband in January 1993. In between those years, the two became affectionately known as Mammy and Pappy. The union produced ten children. They are Violet, Irsiline, Zelminica, Glendora, Carmelda, Judith, Neta, Orson, Patrick and me Nigel.

The combinations of wife, mother, service to the church and a deep belief in God would be the vehicle that drove her with much passion for her entire life. Mammy was a woman of enormous inner strength, who stood steadfastly with her husband amidst life's trials and tribulations. When one storm was over, she would give thanks to God for everything, for she strongly believed that God in her own words "was in the midst of everything".

Mammy would have wanted us to express our sorrows, but not be burdened by her passing. She was quick to say that God had blessed her with a long life and had allowed her to see many things.

In the last twenty years and more so in the last ten years of her life, Mammy travelled extensively to Europe and North America. She visited her children and grandchildren. When she visited Canada four years ago, I took her to church. When she saw people of all races and ethnic backgrounds worshipping and praising God, she simply said "this is how God wanted it to be." It pleased me greatly to see her mingle and speak with the people with relative ease.

Two years ago, we gathered in Boston for a granddaughter wedding and Mammy was very happy. She danced most of the evening showing more energy than I did. She had this glow on her face that spoke volumes about how she felt. I believe this is one way that she would like to be remembered. In addition, I believe she would like to be remembered as someone who fought the good fight, someone who overcame obstacles and someone who stuck through thick and thin with her husband and children. Most of all I believe she would want to be remembered as someone who believed deeply in God and in the teachings of Jesus Christ.

I saw Mammy three weeks ago, my siblings and I all gathered to see her. She was ill, weak, and had difficulty speaking. She was visibly impaired and her memory came and went again, but her indomitable spirit that deep belief in God was apparent. During that visit, a prayer service was held on her behalf. Throughout the service she lipped the songs we sang, and clapped her hands, demonstrating that she was aware of the proceedings. I was told that in the last days of her life, she requested some of her favorite songs to be sung and her requests were met.

When I left after that visit three weeks ago, I knew she was at peace with herself and God. She was contented and comfortable she was ready to meet God.

To my family and to Mammy's friends, please be comforted with the knowledge that Mammy's work on earth is over. She is going to be reunited with her beloved Pappy to prepare and await our own coming.

May this bring you comfort, and may she rest in peace.

Pastor T. N. Walcott then preached the gospel. His sermon was entitled "Keep your eyes on the prize". For his Bible reading reference, he chose two Corinthians 4:18 of the King James Version. With his glasses affixed, he read with purpose in every line

"So we fix our eyes not on what is seen, but on what is unseen. For what is seen is temporary, but what is unseen is eternal".

He said Mammy had set her eyes from an early age on the prize of the eternal. She knew that one day she would have to stand before God for her final reckoning. With that knowledge, she ordered her life for that encounter. He said a wise person would not invest everything in something temporary. A wise person invests in something that will last. He urged the audience to think long term and prepare for their day of reckoning.

After the service at Mile and a Quarter was completed, the funeral cortege moved to All Saints Anglican Church for a second service and interment.

The presiding priest The Reverend Stephen Thorne led the procession of pallbearers from the back of the church to the front of the sanctuary. Reading from the Book of Common Prayer, he said

"I am the resurrection and the life, saith the Lord: he that believeth in me, though he were dead, yet shall he live and whosoever liveth and believeth in me shall never die St. John 11. 25, 26.

The service started immediately with the hymn "Standing on the promises of God."

Standing on the promises of Christ my King
Through eternal ages, let his praises ring
Glory in the highest, I will shout and sing

Standing on the promises of God
Standing, standing, standing on the promises of God,
my Saviour
Standing, standing, I'm standing on the promises
of God.

After the song was rendered, Reverend Thorne invited Mammy's granddaughter Pastor Dr. Verlyn Waterman– Taylor to deliver the homily. She chose Job1: 21 from The New King James version of the Bible - The LORD gave and the LORD has taken away; may the name of the LORD be praised."

Then her sermon began in earnest, she said.

"I know this is a tough verse but, God gave us Mammy; a wonderful gift, a gift that shared her life with all who encountered her, and now he has taken her away. Mammy has left us a blueprint on how we should live our lives. Her love for her children and grandchildren were genuine. She showed compassion in every word or act especially when problems arose. This compassion was for everyone, her children and grandchildren, members of her church family and the community at large. Her devotion to her husband in every aspect of his life teaches us that oaths or promises must be always kept. Mammy loved to go to church and worship, she loved to sing, and she sang in the choir for most of her life. I recall her telling me that I should sing with purpose and meaning. Mammy sang with meaning in every word of the song. She believed that the words were inspired by God and should be sung to their fullest meaning. I believe that she has moved on and will be reunited with her beloved Pappy. May she rest in the everlasting arms of God, and may unspeakable joy await her in heaven.

The attributes I mentioned in this homily were all gifts from God that she shared with us all. We were all blessed by these gifts, and I urge you to emulate the life she lived. So finally, we can say with Job: "The Lord gave, and the Lord has taken away, blessed be the name of the Lord."

The ceremony then moved to the gravesite where Reverend Thorne committed her body to the ground.

Reading from the Book of Common Prayer, he said

"O God, who by the glorious resurrection of your Son Jesus Christ destroyed death and brought life and immortality to light, Grant that your servant Myrtle, being raised with Christ, may know the strength of his presence and rejoice in his eternal glory; who with you and the Holy Spirit lives and reigns, one God, for ever and ever. Amen."

As the grave preparers covered the grave, those gathered sang the hymn "Blessed be the tide that binds," verses one and four are entered here:

> *Blest Be the Tie That Binds*
> *Our Hearts in Christian Love;*
> *The Fellowship of Kindred Minds*
> *Is Like to That Above.*
> *When We Asunder Part,*
> *It Gives Us Inward Pain;*
> *But We Shall Still Be Joined in Heart,*
> *And Hope to Meet Again.*

Mammy's sojourn had ended, unlike Pappy she had started at All Saints and ended at All Saints. With the grave covered and adorned with flowers, some people lingered and some slowly walked away. People stayed on the premises of the church to talk and greet folk they had not seen for many years.

CHAPTER 16

Special Honors - The Service to Unveil Plaques / The Service to Rename the Church

The Service to Unveil Plaques

D ecember 11, 1994 was a typically bright and sunny day on the island of Barbados. On this day, the Mile and a Quarter Pentecostal House of Prayer unveiled a plaque in Pappy's memory. Pappy's beloved Mammy unveiled his plaque in the front sanctuary of the church to tumultuous applause. The plaque was unveiled during a Sunday Community worship.

After many upbeat songs of joy and thanksgiving, the congregation readied itself for the day's sermon. His daughter Pastor Zelminica Skeete preached the sermon. Her sermon was on the theme, Commitment. She chose Luke Chapter 9 verse 62 as her Bible text, "No one who puts a hand to the plow and looks back is fit for service in the kingdom of God." She said Pappy had committed his life to serve God, and he served God, and this church with an unremitting commitment. She said the plaque would "remind all that enter this sanctuary that Pappy was committed to God and the people that worshipped in this building." She said, "He never wavered from those commitments." She told those present that, "their commitment to serve God should also be unceasing." As we go forward let us be ever mindful of our commitments to God and also those around us."

A plaque was also unveiled for Mammy in November 2000. As was the case with Pappy, this plaque was unveiled during a Sunday morning church service. Pastor Zelminica Skeete unveiled and blessed the plaque. The Church leaders had the plaque erected adjacent to Pappy's plaque. The plaque acknowledged that she was a founding member who served for fifty-five unbroken years. Pastor Skeete recalled that, "Mammie always stood beside her husband in the good and bad times. She said her life was an example of commitment, love and service. For those reasons, we had no choice we had to place the plaques together."

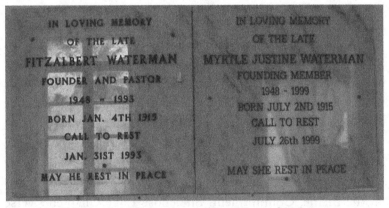

Side by side - Plaques in memory of Pappy & Mammy

The Service to Rename the Church

The church Pappy started in 1944 honored him again in 1995. This time the congregation voted overwhelmingly to rename the church "The Fitz Albert Waterman Memorial Pentecostal Church." Throughout his life, he had repeatedly stated that the church belonged to the people of Mile and a Quarter. With this gesture, the people of Mile and a Quarter were honoring his contribution to the well-being of the community. They were ensuring his name remained recognizable with their community for as long as the community existed.

This ceremony was a service of joy and thanksgiving for his life and service to the people of Mile and a Quarter. Pastor Zelminica Skeete, the church's Pastor, invited former members, and other elderly saints who knew and worshipped with Pappy at various times in their lives.

Pastor Zelminica Skeete Pappy's daughter,
became Pastor after his passing

Those in attendance sang lustily and some danced to the rhythms of guitars and drums. The rendition of this song towards the end of the singing section of the service, helped to maintain the joyful atmosphere for the remainder of the service.

Stand up, stand up for Jesus,
Ye soldiers of the cross;
Lift high his royal banner,
It must not suffer loss.
From victory unto victory
His army shall he lead
Till every foe is vanquished,
And Christ is Lord indeed.

When the singing section of the service was finished, people gave testimonies. Some said that Pappy provided assistance when they were in need. Others thanked God for gifting them a man whose very presence commanded respect from all. Two former elderly members said when he preached, you could see the anointing pouring out of him. They said a glow appeared around his head during sermons.

Evangelist Carlotta Cumberbatch was a founding member of the church and testified at the renaming service. She said, "I came to church one Wednesday night for a service and he was sitting alone at the front of the church. As I grew closer, I saw what I would call a bright light around his head. I stopped because I first thought something was wrong. I then drew closer, and the light was still there, and I said Pastor, Pastor are you okay? He was startled as if I had awakened him from a deep sleep. He said he was fine and was waiting for the saints to start the service. That sight of the bright light around him has remained with me all these years and will be with me until the end."

Pastor T.N. Walcott preached the sermon. He chose to speak on the topic "Working for the Master" He chose for his Bible text, Hebrews 6:10. "God is not unjust; he will not forget your work and the love you have shown him as you have helped his people and continue to help them." Pastor Walcott stressed that God does not forget our work and honors us accordingly. He said, "Therefore we believers of God could not forget the work of Pastor Waterman.

We have a duty to honor the work he did for God and the people of God today." He said, "Future generations will come to this church and learn of the sterling work of the Pastor for God's kingdom and for God's people. We should continue to rejoice long after this service is over for the work Pastor Waterman did to enhance God's work, in this church and this community of Mile and a Quarter as a whole."

Pastor Debra Worrell Pappy's granddaughter – The present Pastor
Became Pastor after the passing of her mother Pastor Skeete

CHAPTER 17

Final Thoughts
and Tributes

People, who knew Pappy and were familiar with his work, have repeatedly asked many questions. One of them was how could a man thrown out of school at age seven have the confidence and foresight to lead people, some with higher educational achievements? Why was he, never challenged as Pastor of the Mile and a Quarter Pentecostal House of Prayer? They have all concluded that he was simply great in administering the church and excellent in his sermons. Other questions asked included, how could a man starting so low on the totem pole rise so high in the minds of people, and influence his community in the manner that he did?

Those that asked questions of Pappy acknowledged that God gave him gifts in many aspects. He had a photographic memory; he knew the Bible and interpreted it with accuracy. He had a presence that commanded respect and attention especially when he spoke. He was humble and had the ability to listen intently to others when they unfurled their burdens. Some also said that he was physically handsome.

The question asked by his children was, how could his parents and grandparents who were literate and saw the benefits literacy brought, not provide the funds for him to go to school? His three other siblings also suffered his fate.

I have also asked these questions. If Pappy had a formal education, how would his life evolve? Would his life have evolved in much the same way in terms of his devotion to God. Would he have made service to God not only his calling, but also his profession? Would he have established other churches around the island of Barbados and perhaps in other Caribbean countries? Would he have organized a grouping of churches under an umbrella with full time administrators? Would he have used his practical understanding as an organizer, to set up a college to train people in the various disciplines in the Ministries of Jesus Christ?

Pappy had good hand skills; he owned a few mason's trowels, a saw, hammer and a measuring tape amongst other tools. He used those tools to complete many projects around the house and church. For work around the house, Pappy constructed animal enclosures, and erected a fence in his backyard.

If Pappy had a formal education, would he have developed these skills? Would he have become a master mason or carpenter? Would he have evolved into a builder, with the ability to draw building plans?

Answers for these questions are far from simple. We will never know. However, an analysis of his life's story suggests, that he could have achieved greater goals with a formal education. Having lived with him for twenty- eight years, I can attest to the following. Pappy was ambitious, possessed a thirst for knowledge, intensely passionate, forward thinking and saw the overall picture of an issue. He was great at managing money and practiced budgeting. He possessed a keen insight into people around him and those that he encountered.

With a formal education, Pappy's confidence would have been greater than it was. This confidence would have allowed him to negotiate with the power brokers of his society. It would have allowed him to canvas for donations to start other projects that revolved around the community and the church. It would have allowed him to navigate with greater ease many issues on his own. I believe his advocacy for Christ would have been wider. I believe that he would have been a household name in Barbados for the gifts of his beautiful voice and its use in Apologetics.

People have argued that God wanted him to be pure, untouched by dogma, a diamond in the rough. There is a school of thought that people trained in theology, are generally not filled with the Holy Ghost. In addition, the belief exist that they study too much manufactured philosophical thought. The Holy Ghost poured out of Pappy, when he preached.

Pappy loved to travel, he and his beloved Mammy travelled to England, where they visited several historic sites. They also visited places of interest in the North American cities of New York, Boston and Toronto. I believe if Pappy disposable income was greater, his travels would have been extensive.

Pappy & Mammy London, England, 1983

For about 25 years of his life, Pappy was literate. His primary educational sources were oral. With the advent of radio and then television, he was able to listen to sermons and speeches. For sermons, he listened to the American, Pastor R W Schambach late on Sunday nights on radio in the 1970's. In the 1980's he listened to Bishop Granville Williams a Barbadian preacher who also was on air on Sunday nights. When he attended functions whether funerals or weddings, he listened intently to the priest's exhortations, and came home to discuss them with Mammy.

On radio and then television, he also listened to the news and absorbed debates on issues of current affairs. These sources improved his vocabulary and widened his perspective of life around him. Influenced in part by these new sources of information, Pappy added issues of current affairs to his sermons. What is noteworthy is that he remembered everything heard with his photographic memory.

As for his writing, he practiced intently to be proficient. In the beginning, once comfortable with this skill he wrote his name and showed it to his children. He asked for opinions on the formation of the letters. He advanced to writing the topics for sermons, and sentences that he wanted to emphasize for these sermons. He also practiced writing letters, which were mainly introspective, thought-provoking pieces.

His reading was laborious, this was caused by the fact that as a beginner he read material geared to experience readers. Despite the challenges faced, Pappy persisted. He finished a Bible verse, then a paragraph, page, and eventually a chapter.

On many occasions, people requested Pappy to speak on occasions that were important to the people who asked. On June 28, 1986, he spoke at the wedding of this writer.

"I am pleased to speak at my son's wedding it is indeed a blessing that this day has arrived for him and the entire Waterman family. I want to start by reminding you that love is of God and God is love. The Apostle Paul in Corinthians 1, Chapter 13 tell us that, "If you have faith that can move mountains, but do not have love, you are nothing."

Whoever does not love, does not know God, because God is love. Proverbs 18:22 tells us "That he who finds a wife finds what is good and receives favor from the LORD." I just wanted to show that marriage is divine and pleasing in the eyes of God.

God also ordains marriage, for the growth and extension of the family. It allows for the continuation of the family with babies. Children also help to cement marriages in many ways. The importance of families increases with children.

I have been married for 51 years and I am still going strong. You just must have understanding and be wise in how you conduct your life. Without understanding and wisdom, someone could step in and corrupt your life, and leave your household stranded. You must acknowledge God in your life if you do not; that is a mistake.

My advice to Nigel is that you must always respect your wife and restrain from abuse of every manner. To Hazel, you must follow suit. Remember marriage is a union, and your thoughts and actions should include your spouse. I urge you to live in love and acknowledge God in your daily living."

Pappy & Mammy at my wedding - June 28, 1986

CHAPTER 18

The Verdict of Those Who Sat at Pappy's Feet

H is children called him PAPPY. Members of his congregation, including the youth, called him Pastor or Pastor Waterman. I have never heard anyone call him Fitz Albert.

Pastor Waterman was an amazing man. You could always tell when he was in your midst. He commanded respect by his presence alone, whether in the Church or in the street. What added to the amazement of this man was the way he presented the 'Word of God' on Sundays. Pappy knew every Book of the Bible. He had the ability to refer to various Bible passages in the Old and New Testaments to support whatever sermon he was preaching. He would say to the congregation at the beginning of the Sermon 'turn with me to (a chosen passage of the Bible)". He would call on someone to read the chosen passage. Then he would exhort on the many verses, pulling passages from other Books of the Bible to support his sermon. So focused was the congregation that there was hardly a voice heard (except for the occasional Amen and Hallelujah), or a movement in the Church.

It was usual for Preachers to call for a song of invitation at the end of the sermon so that persons in the congregation could make their way to the altar. I had the privilege of hearing Pastor Waterman preach a sermon at a Revival Service and before the Sermon was finished, persons in the congregation were making their way to the altar. So powerful was the sermon.

Fitz Albert "Pappy" Waterman – a great Man of God, a powerful preacher, a respected and respectable figure in the community. An amazing Human Being.

With highest Regards
Haynesley Benn.

***

I became friends with my neighbor's daughter Neta when I moved to St. Peter in the 1960's. She was Pastor Waterman's daughter, and she invited me to church. During a revival service, I gave my life to the Lord. He became my first Pastor and I say without hesitation, my foundation in Christ. This started me on a true Christian journey. On Sunday mornings, Pastor Waterman called a young person in the church to read the Bible text and then he would preach. When he preached it felt like he was preaching directly to me, and I would tremble. I often wondered how he knew what he was saying to me or about me. I wondered who could have told him that I did something wrong.

He always encouraged the youth in the church, he always pushed us to excel. He loved the youth and defended most of their actions. I remember well how he got Sister Aldeane started into her ministry. In fact, she went on to Bible College. He also defended Shernell Toppin. The church had a dress code in place, and Shernell wore an earring, which violated this code. Pastor Cumberbatch told her to desist from fellowship, and Pappy asked Pastor Cumberbatch to be more lenient in his enforcement of the dress code.

The youth at the church were very dynamic and we could perform in most genres. When we performed by singing and reciting Christian poetry and Bible verses at other churches; especially those without a choir or Sunday school, we were envied.

At Bible study, he would encourage the young ones to share their thoughts. We did not always get it right, but Pastor Waterman was always ready to interpret; and he gave a background to the topic we were discussing. This is where my Bible education started; this is where my knowledge of God grew, because of this man of God. He did not have a PhD, but his knowledge, his photographic memory, the ability to recall information, his faith and confidence was something to behold. I strongly believe that the Holy Spirit led him at all times. I am sure of this because he did not read the Bible, yet he possessed this empirical knowledge of its content.

He would preach sermons and they would be so powerful, that people would flock to the altar to receive prayer. I also know that many literally trembled in their boots at his every word. As a result, of his preaching, many came to know and believe in Christ. Several of these people became born again Christians, because of his sermons. He was an excellent preacher. Without hesitation, I will say again that the Holy Spirit led him every step of the way.

I am grateful to God for his life and for bringing him into my life. He will be forever in my heart and memories. I speak of him whenever I get the opportunity to do so, especially in church settings. I can still recall the words he recited before he prayed before the congregation. I find myself repeating them nowadays before I pray. They are as follows:

> *How sweet the name of Jesus sounds*
> *In a believer's ear!*
> *It soothes his sorrows, heals his wounds,*
> *And drives away his fear.*
> *It makes the wounded spirit whole*
> *And calms the troubled breast;*
> *'Tis manna to the hungry soul,*
> *And to the weary, rest.*

> *I pray that he is resting peacefully in the loving arms of Jesus.*

Sister Pat Eastmond

***

His peers knew Fitz Albert Waterman as Pastor Fitz Waterman but to us his children, and me a great niece, we dared not call the patriarch of our family none other than Pappy. For us he was the one we looked to for guidance.

All my life I have known Pappy to be a Christian. Pappy's entire life was Christ like. He lived so much with that in mind, and in his daily living, you did not have to read your Bible to envisage the peaceful and fulfilling life of a Christian.

One striking charm about the old man was the fact that he never saw your color, or your face. His heart always went ahead of him, and he saw need. I learned later in life that his qualities were from his childhood. For me, it has been the one part of his life I have loved, lived and practiced since my Sunday school days.

Pastor Waterman saw people and not their sin. He saw the person and not the wrong that they did. This was, in my opinion, the main reason why he was so well loved. Both young and older folks gravitated towards him. Of course, this made his counselling easier than normal. He took the time to talk to you and not down to you.

I remember Pappy as not only the father of his household but for the village. You were not only invited to pass by, but to come in. Most of the folks walked with their small children but the adults saw the Christ like life he lived and many cherished the thought of their children having him rest his hand on their head or even them sitting on his knees like in the days of Jesus. On such occasions, as adults we would be reminded of the children's Bible story "when mothers of Salem brought their children to Jesus" Matthew 19:14

As the pastor of Mile and a Quarter Pentecostal House of Prayer, Pastor Waterman made the sanctuary a welcoming place and a place of comfort.

Pastor Waterman presided over the time when revival for the church meant one week of prayer meetings and two weeks of other churches visiting our church. In those revival services, genuine

Christians renewed their faith, and quite often they also experienced a true visit from the Holy Spirit

It was also the time that most unbelievers made the time to become faith believers. During this time, sinners and saints came together. Pastor Waterman went on a special drive to see sinners brought to Christ.

When we visited churches, we travelled by pick-up truck for day or night services. When we travelled by pick-up trucks, Pastor Waterman would let you know travel fare or no travel fare you are invited to join for the service. His mantra was, "come let us go and fellowship with our brothers and sisters."

Pastor Waterman kept serving God and leading sinners to Christ as his priorities until he died. It was felt among some believers that he was a modern day, Moses. I remember quite well the day he was laid to rest. Emotions ran high that day and people reflected on a life lived for God. It took my thoughts back to Enoch and Elijah, and how they lived their lives. It was then and there that I asked God to let me be part of his kingdom.

In concluding, I can most assuredly say through our beloved Pastor Waterman Christ like life, many souls have been born into God's eternal kingdom. May he rest in Glory.

Sister Margaret Bovell

Index

1. The Panama Canal

2. History of Barbados: From Wikipedia, the free encyclopedia

3. Churches of Barbados

4. Journal of Pan African Studies, 2021

5. A case for Reparations in the Caribbean, Kaden Lashley, May 01, 2021

6. /www.nytimes.com/2022/01/04/world/canada/Canada

7. Barbados Succession Act, Cap. 249

8. https://www.catholicnewsagency.com/news/248633/despite-millions-in-catholic

9. https://www.bing.com/search?q=what+is+the+third+gang+as+in+caribbean+plantations&form

10. Melodies of Praise – Editor Edwin P Anderson – Publisher: Gospel Publishing House, Springfield, Missouri, 1957

11. Songs of Joy and Gladness – Editors W Mc Donald, Joshua Gill, Jno R Sweeney, W.J. Kirkpatrick --- Publisher: Mc Donald and Gill

12. I come to the garden alone was composed in 1912 by C Austin Miles (1868-1946)

13. https://www.google.ca/search?q=speeches+by+haile+selassie&ie=UTF-8&oe=UTF-8&hl=en- ca&client=safari

14. It is well with my soul – Words by Horatio Spafford

15. https://www.google.com/url?sa=t&rct=j&q=&esrc=s &source=web&cd=&cad=rja&uact=8&ved=2ahUKE wjTwPfa9qn8AhXflnIEHeL7BegQFnoECCUQAQ& url=https%3A%2F%2Fwww.faithandworship.com%2 FHarvest_Thanksgiving_Resources_and_Prayers.htm &usg=AOvVaw0_OM2MA_f2-HQ-mbjcP4dY

16. https://www.google.ca/url?sa=t&rct=j&q=&esrc=s&s ource=web&cd=&ved=2ahUKEwie6p6_9Kn8AhUD hHIEHcH5AvYQFnoECCwQAQ&url=https%3A%2 F%2Fwww.barbadospocketguide.com%2Four-island- barbados%2Fheritage%2Fthe-story-of- sugar.html&usg=AO vVaw0Wkydh5B_tsFtqXPze8R ue

17. We Plow the Fields and Scatter > Lyrics | Matthias Claudius. 1782

18. When we all get to heaven – Written by Eliza E Hewitt, 1898

19. And can it be – Written by Charles Wesley 1738

20. Book of Common Prayers

21. Each Step I take – Written by Elmo Mercer

22. Is this not the Land of Beulah – Written by William Hunter, 1898

23. Standing on the Promises of God – Written by Russell Kelso Carter 1886

24. Blest be the ties that bind – Written by John Fawcett 1782

Printed in the United States
by Baker & Taylor Publisher Services

Printed in the United States
by Baker & Taylor Publisher Services